ALENE

Alene: Chevron's First African-American Scientist

ISBN 978-0-578-56568-2

Published by Noahs Ark Publishing Service
www.noahsarkpublishing.com

Edited by Lisa Beasley
Graphic Design by Tabia Clinkscales, www.tabiaclinkscales.com

To Jennifer Hudson
4-11-2024

ALENE

CHEVRON'S FIRST AFRICAN-AMERICAN SCIENTIST

May God Bless you +
Happy Mothers Day
We Love you and "Never
Gene up."

ALENE BROWN HARRIS

Alene Brown Harris

Noahs Ark Publishing Service
Beverly Hills, California

DEDICATION

To my mother, Eula Lee Brown-Hill: You are my biggest and best supporter and a champion at showing your love, admiration, and selflessness to me. To my husband, Bennie Harris: Your love, sacrifice, and complete devotion never goes unnoticed. Thank you seems inadequate to describe how grateful I am for your support throughout the years. Nakita and Shanta, my loving daughters, you both continually inspire me. I love you beyond expression. Thank you for giving me two beautiful grandchildren, Asiah and Isaiah. Lastly, I thank God for loving me and ordering my steps throughout this journey.

CONTENTS

ACKNOWLEDGEMENTS

To the late Lacey Hill, my inspiration, I don't know how I would have made it without you.

Thank you, T.C. May. Dad, though we met late in life, our making up for lost time has left an indelible mark. Thank you for sharing your life with me.

I am grateful for my late grandparents, Dan Wheeler, Lena and Leon May, and Ellen and Dan Brown, for loving me and weaving their positive influence into my soul's fabric.

Thank you to my siblings, Johnnie Mae, Daniel, Billy, Lorean, Michael, and Melvin, for your love and thoughtfulness throughout the years. Johnnie Mae, thank you for exposing me to many positive things in life.

Special recognition goes to my Aunt Ruby, Uncle Jessie Garner, and Mary Nell for their encouragement and deliberate insistence, which motivated me to work at Chevron.

Additional honor is given to my nieces, nephews, cousins, aunts, uncles, and extended family members.

To my Chevron family: Thank you, Joe Novack. Your persistence changed my life forever. Dick Richardson and Nolan Goodman, you taught me everything I needed to begin my journey as a laboratory scientist. Hugh Holland, you remain an integral part of my destiny. Dennis H. Ofcacek, you were an excellent boss and friend. You all will never be forgotten.

Thank you to my good friends, Alice, Karen, Diane, and Paulette, for standing by me at the beginning of my career as a scientist.

Thank you Castro Photography Studios.

Sharon, my friend, thank you for your wisdom, encouragement, and feedback.

Laval Belle and Noahs Ark Publishing, thank you for the opportunity to express myself and share my story.

INTRODUCTION

We are born into this world as a clean slate. Without a blemish or stain, we travel through the birth canal, away from our warm, safe environment into a stark, bright, new world. Our first gasp of air tunnels through to our lungs, life on the outside commences, and our slates begin to wear our stories.

It's a good thing we don't know, and aren't able to predict, what lies ahead at this stage of the game. If it were possible, we might certainly entertain the thought of crawling back into the safe haven we once knew. The thought of experiencing trauma, fear, rejection, illness, and pain, mixed with moments of pleasure, is not at all appealing. Though appearing to some to be simply a necessary evil, experiencing hardship often creates conquerors, leaders, and proverbial kings. With all humility, I can proudly say that I stand amongst these brave leaders and overcomers.

I have fallen, been knocked down for the count, and been left for dead. But I can now proclaim to anyone that, when life knocks you down, you can get up, brush yourself off, and try again—as many times as it takes to get it right. No matter what others may think about you, it is important to remember that the prescription for survival is: to stay focused on your goals, no matter what happens, and stand firm in your convictions.

I feel incredible. I can finally share my life experiences with you. All of my ups and downs now have freedom of expression on these pages.

CHAPTER ONE

HOME GROWN

My roots are deeply embedded in the South—specifically Mississippi. During slavery, Mississippi was commonly known as one of the largest slave states, along with Virginia, North Carolina, South Carolina, and Maryland. Most of its economy was structured around plantation agriculture, and cotton was the undisputed king of Mississippi's vast farming economy.

After the Civil War, Mississippi's economic growth stemmed from the work of freed slaves who continued to clear land to develop farms. As they continued to labor in the fields, some of them would eventually become owners of the land. A time came when many of the farms were owned by black farmers. Unfortunately, many of those farmers ended up losing their farms in the 1930s and 1940s because of natural causes, the price of cotton dropping, and the steady growth of racial hatred. Mississippi became a racial hotbed during the Civil Rights Movement, and many African-American and civil-rights leaders who stood up for the cause tragically lost their lives.

Despite the many horrific and tumultuous events suffered in Mississippi during that time, the state was home to many who contributed to America's rich culture: civil rights leaders like Charles and Medgar Evers, actor James Earl Jones, blues icons B.B. King and Muddy Waters, songstress Leontyne Price, writer Richard Wright, and the multifaceted mogul Oprah Winfrey, to name a few. (Infoplease.com)

The town of Jayess, Mississippi, was named after J.S. Butterfield, a lumber magnate who owned Butterfield Lumber Company. His initials, J.S., were used until the postal service opened in 1912 and changed the town's name from J.S. to Jayess. The town of Jayess also had a sawmill and a cotton gin, and a Ku Klux Klan's klavern was established there in the early 1960s.

My name and ancestry are not hailed over the world, yet I consider my lineage of great value. In spite of challenges thrown in our paths and the great hardships we endured, my family thrived. We have lived and continue to live our best lives, having made our own significant contributions in the communities we were predestined to occupy.

My parents are Eula Lee Brown and T.C. May. My mother was delivered by a midwife on January 6, 1923, at 9:00 a.m., in Jayess, Mississippi. Her mother's name was Addie Brown. She died when my mother was only 5 years old. Her father was Dan Wheeler. Mom was raised by her grandparents, Dan and Ellen Brown, at Aunt Martha's home, in Monticello, Mississippi. They lived in a typical small, Southern, country house. The bedroom was in the front room. If you were looking in from the front door, you would see a full-size bed and a shift-row dresser for storing clothes. Looking to the right, in that same room, was a huge fireplace and a rocking chair that Aunt Martha sat in each day. Sitting next to the wall was a gigantic trunk, where Aunt Martha kept her clothes. She never wanted anyone to touch or go near her trunk.

There was a door leading to the kitchen, which housed a very old wood-burning stove with four burner tops for cooking. We often walked through the woods to find branches for that stove and the fireplace, then brought them back to the house and stacked them in a corner. At night, I slept with my grandmother Ellen whenever possible, and I loved waking up and seeing the reflection on the ceiling of the fire burning in the fireplace. I remember that my grandfather Dan used to roast sweet potatoes under the ashes after the fire died down, and he would also hide pint bottles of whiskey under the cold ashes for buyers who dropped by to purchase them. But we had no idea at the time that he was into bootlegging.

My name is Alene Brown, born the second eldest of six children, on September 8, 1948, and like my mother, I was delivered by a midwife, in the same small town of Jayess, Mississippi. My parents never married. My father was a mystery to me for many years. He was born in Ruth, Mississippi in Lincoln County. His mother was Lena Thompson, and his father was Leon May (also from Lincoln County). My grandmother

Lena was a school teacher, and her family managed to own an estate of 20 acres in Brookhaven, Mississippi, that's been handed down from generation to generation. Anyone could live on the land, but it can never be sold. I discovered this information just recently, since I was not raised by my biological father, and my relatives didn't readily share it.

I didn't meet my father until 1993 when I was almost 45 years old. My cousin Clifton Stovall, who was living in California at the time, mentioned to me that my father had moved to Jackson, Mississippi. I asked Clifton to call my father and let him know that I wanted to meet him. Clifton was always in constant contact with family members.

During that time, my husband, Ben, and I had traveled from Los Angeles to Birmingham for his family reunion, and little did I know that my father's family was having a family reunion in Gadsden, Alabama, during the same time. But I found out that Dad, aka Pops, didn't attend. I was so disappointed. But Clifton gave me my dad's address, so Ben and I drove to Jackson, Mississippi, to visit him. We arrived in the afternoon, and I was quite nervous. The magic moment was about to take place. When I saw him, I walked up to him, and he gave me a great, big hug! Whew! What a beautiful relief!

He was petite, and I could sense that he was extremely nervous, too. He took Ben and me to his sitting room, and we talked, and talked, and talked! We spent the night right there at his home, got up the next morning, and went to Shoney's for breakfast. My dad and Ben hit it off well, and a bonding relationship formed between them.

When it was time for us to leave Jackson for Los Angeles later that afternoon, I really hated to go, but we had jobs to return to. You would have thought I had won a billion-dollar jackpot because I had finally met my birth father after so many years. I was filled with pure joy, and gratitude was flowing from my heart. Oh, happy day! My dad and I continued to call each other every week to say hello and make up for the time we'd lost.

§

I come from a family of sharecroppers and domestic housekeepers. We didn't have much money, but we were rich in love! My grandma Ellen died when I was 10 years old. Her death was so painful to me that it made me want to die, too. Our bond was so very strong. She always had something extra saved for my older sister, Johnnie Mae, and me under her bed, in a large dishpan. I could not wait to see what she had hidden away from others just for us.

My grandfather was the "godfather," or "kingpin," of the family. He controlled everything and everyone. All of us had to do whatever he said. Right after I was born, my father wanted my mother to come with him to Milwaukee, Wisconsin, but my grandfather said no! He was afraid that my father would mistreat my mother, and she would be too far away from him to protect her.

My mother married twice (to two different men) and had more children with both husbands. Adrian Daniel came along during my mother's marriage to David Pittman. Then Bill, Michael, and Lorean were born when my mother was married to her second husband, Lacy Hill. My mother married Lacy in 1955 when we were very young children. He was an extraordinary man—loving, kind, thoughtful, and absolutely remarkable!

My mother was the disciplinarian in our home. Back in the day, she disciplined us with whippings and spankings. She'd use a broom, stick, belt, tree limb, or whatever she could quickly get her hands on. Often, when we misbehaved, Mom would slap us across the face so hard and fast that we didn't know we were hit until our faces began to sting from the impact. I never liked spankings. Besides being painful, they always left marks and scars on my body. So, whatever my mother asked of me, I tried extremely hard to comply with. My sister Johnnie was the complete opposite of me and couldn't have cared less about being disciplined. Day after day, she would get a spanking without even blinking her eyes and then continue doing whatever she wanted to do. But Johnnie could never leave our home without me. We always had to travel together because Mom was afraid Johnnie might get in trouble.

Sometimes our mother would punish us by making us stand in a corner, face a wall, and stand on one foot for an undetermined amount of time. It always seemed like forever. If we got caught allowing our foot to touch the floor, the time was doubled, tripled, or made even longer! These forms of discipline may appear harsh to many today, but it was part of our culture back then, and my siblings and I are still alive today. These punishments were not considered criminal, but rather, were respected and accepted as the norm.

Because my Johnnie couldn't go anywhere unless I accompanied her, I believe she resented me. She wanted to go on a decent date with her boyfriend without me looking at her back and returning home to report everything to our mother. I must say, I was a tattletale. I told everything! My mom made me responsible for Johnnie, so there was a little extra pressure on my part. When we went out, I had to make sure nothing happened to Johnnie. Of course, my mother didn't have to worry. She knew I was scared of everything and wouldn't do anything wrong because she had put fear in me. But Johnnie was a little daredevil. You'd tell her not to do something, and she did it anyway, just for the heck of it. She didn't mind suffering the consequences, but I did!

I remember my mother being such a strong hard-working woman. She loved gardening, planting vegetables, and raising chickens and hogs. After attending college and moving from Mississippi to California, I used to come home to visit earlier than usual and stay a few extra days just to help her in her garden. She loves beautiful flowers and plants, and on my recent visit in July 2019, I made sure I checked and pruned her plants, buying extra feed for them and taking the time to add fertilizer, etc. This has been a routine of mine for the past forty years.

My mom's second husband, Lacy Hill, felt that Mom should learn how to drive so she wouldn't have to depend on him to take her around town. So, he frequently encouraged her to get under the wheel. However, one night, as she was driving home, she actually forgot how to use the brakes on the car and almost hit a house head-on. She panicked and scared everyone in the car with her. She quickly made the decision, right then and there, that it was time to stop driving. Mom has not driven a car since then, and that was sixty years ago.

My mom was driven by the desire to see her children lead successful lives. She constantly brought Johnnie into her bedroom for pep talks. Johnnie would listen to her wisdom and warnings against having children out of wedlock and how she was treated differently after being robbed of her virginity. She talked about sex in raw terms and told graphic stories about childbirth. Of course, that nearly scared me to death. She said, "You CANNOT bring a baby in this house and expect us to help you raise it." Mom had me so scared that I didn't want a boyfriend at all! Through most of high school, I avoided boys. I didn't want to talk to them, and I had no desire to go on a date. However, during my senior year, around prom time, I invited a guy to my house. My mother had a strict curfew. All male guests had to leave the premises by 10:00 p.m. If I hadn't ushered my guest to the door by that time, she would go into the kitchen and start banging pots and pans on the table. With each passing minute, the noise would get louder and louder. I learned to avoid this by having him leave at least 10 minutes before curfew. I did not want my mother to embarrass me.

My sister and I were so naïve back then. It wasn't until years later that we discovered a hole in my mother's bedroom wall that was directly across from the sitting area where we entertained boys. She was watching our every move through that peephole. If those boys tried to touch or kiss us, she would bang a pot or skillet against the wall. We can all laugh about it now, but back then, the sound was tremendously frightening.

My mom's sister Ruby didn't have any children, so she helped raise us. Daniel, Johnnie, and I were the eldest children and her favorites. Although Aunt Ruby always wanted children of her own, it was not meant to be. She constantly asked my mom if Johnnie Mae and I could stay with her. Mom finally gave in and let us stay with her when Johnnie Mae was 10 and I was 8. We lived with her for two years. Aunt Ruby lived near my mom, so we weren't far away. Occasionally, Mom would dress-up and go down to the local Juke Joint with Aunt Ruby. Mom loved her music.

My Aunt Ruby's husband, Uncle Jessie, always catered to Aunt Ruby. He did exactly what she told him to do— every day, day after day. His nickname for her was "Rubylee Baby." Uncle Jessie was an excellent cook. He had been a cook while he was in the army, and he prepared all the meals. Aunt Ruby never had to cook. He made the best lemonade, using fresh-squeezed lemons from his lemon tree. Aunt Ruby was a bootlegger. She sold whiskey and cigarettes, which was her side-hustle business while Uncle Jessie had a gambling problem. He loved to shoot dice and spent a lot of time on his knees throwing out his dice and hoping he'd win the jackpot from the other players in the game. He would play for hours at a time. After being discharged from the army, he worked at a furniture store for a while.

Aunt Ruby was good to us, but she kept us working around her house, and she never let up. That infuriated me. I felt that having time to relax and reflect was needed, but it was hard to have moments like that around Aunt Ruby. But I did love her dearly. She is sorely missed.

Although Daniel's name is officially Adrian Daniel Pittman, our family has always called him Daniel. Out of all my mother's children, he is the only one that didn't graduate from high school. Instead, he started working and brought his pay home to our mother to help with expenses. At age 15, he joined Job Corps and moved to Glide, Oregon. He was the first one in our family to fly in an airplane. Daniel lived in Oregon for about one year then relocated back home to work as a heavy equipment operator.

Daniel was two years younger than I, and he followed me everywhere! When I finally started dating, Mom used to send him right along with me. She'd tell me, "You can go, but ya'll better be back here by 10:00 p.m." So Daniel tagged along with us. But what Mom didn't know is that Daniel had a girlfriend. He and I always came back home together, because if we didn't, we knew Mom was no joke and could hand us our "you know what's" on a platter if we didn't mind her. Aunt Ruby would whip us, too, with anything she got her hands on.

Daniel was rather sneaky while growing up. He would always steal food off my plate by tricking me to look elsewhere while he swiped whatever he wanted. In fact, he still does that to this very day. He thought my plate always looked better than his. He was rebellious too! Mama would put us on the school bus every morning. At the very next stop, Daniel would get off the bus! When Mom tried to whip him, he would run and hide, and he couldn't be caught. He wouldn't come in the house. He would go into the woods and sit next to a tree all night if he felt he was going to get a whipping.

Lorean is the baby girl of the family. Presently, she is the main caretaker of our mother, and she does all the housework. She proudly boasts that she knew how to cook when she 10 years old. Johnnie Mae and I taught her how to cook cornbread as her first dish. The next thing we taught her to cook was a delicious homemade banana pudding.

Lorean ran away from home once, when she was 10 years old. Johnnie Mae had moved to Milwaukie, and I had left for college. We left Lorean home with three brothers, and oh boy, it was a nightmare for her, to say the least. She had to do all the cooking and cleaning by herself. Just imagine, a young girl with three hungry, bothersome, and lazy brothers. They never helped her clean up, so she always felt alone, and it's still somewhat like that today. She likes to say that, in spite of it all, she's made it to 60 years old and survived.

Despite the struggles with responsibilities, Lorean enjoyed being raised by our mother. She often says, "Oooo, she was a tough old woman, and I was a bad girl who always got a whoopin'." We had a chicken house that looked like an old smokehouse. When you walked inside, you'd see the chickens sitting way up high. We also had a dog named Jack. Every time Lorean got in trouble, there was a whoopin' waiting right around the corner. She would run away from Mama and try to hide under the chicken house. But old Jack would catch her every single time before she could squeeze underneath, and Mama was right there, ready to spank her. Still life was good then, and still is, even though it gets tough sometimes. As Lorean puts it, "Hey, that's life."

Lorean never thought she would be the chosen one in our family to take care of our 90-year old mother, but she is now thankful and blessed that she is. My baby sister has sacrificed much of her life. She doesn't get much of a break, but she never misses a beat when it comes to making sure Mom has what she needs. I truly admire Lorean and her selfless contribution to our family.

Billy is my younger brother and is as spoiled as he can be. We have no right to complain about it and can only blame ourselves because we enabled him. I raise my hand as the number-one guilty party on this one. I took care of him all the time when he was a baby. He is quite the character and can always spin a good story. But you'll find out later that Billy was lying or stretching the truth. For years he'll tell you the same story, and every time there's a different angle to it. He is the best storyteller!

Billy is charismatic and charming, and yes, he's a ladies' man. We don't quite understand what they see in him, but they LOVE some Billy Hill! My niece Summer recalls a day when she was three hours away from home, filling up at a gas station. She said:

"This lady asked me, 'Are you Billy Hill's niece?' I was almost afraid to answer the question because of his reputation. The lady went on to say, 'I used to date your uncle back in the day.' This lady was trying to make me remember who she was, and I was thinking to myself, *Do you know how many women Uncle Billy has had? Unless you were one of the main ones around here, I don't know who you are.*"

Billy can be self-centered at times, but all in all, he is a very caring person. Billy is very intelligent, sometimes a little too intelligent for his own good. He doesn't keep promises, and when you send him to the store, you better make sure you give him exact change. Don't even think he's going to bring your change back, whether you give him a five-dollar bill or a hundred-dollar bill. Billy is a hustler by nature. I don't know where he got that hustler mentality from. But one thing I do know for sure is that he didn't get if from our father, because Lacy Hill was a true gentleman.

Michael is my spoiled baby brother, who enjoyed a happy childhood growing up. He loved to help Mom raise the chickens and pigs and work in the garden. He also joined us out there in the cotton fields when he was only 6 years old. Since we didn't have a baby sitter, he learned how to work at a very early age. After graduating from high school, he enlisted in the military and stayed for almost six years. Then he moved back to Mississippi and lived there for five years before moving to Los Angeles to stay with Johnnie Mae and me. Michael was a normal kid who did normal things and got into the normal types of trouble all kids get into. And no, he didn't escape our Mom's whippings either!

I love my brothers and sisters. Yes, we've had the usual sibling rivalries that most families experience. Truthfully speaking, my brothers and sisters were somewhat envious of my relationship with our mother. After I moved out, I would come home and make a big fuss over Mommy. I'd make sure she was comfortable, take her out to eat, and spend my vacation cleaning and watering her flowers and planting trees, and do anything I felt would make her happy. Our relationship has always been strong like that. Growing up, whenever I walked in the house and saw Mom, I'd run straight over to her and smother her with hugs.

Years later, when I'd come home to visit, my siblings would always say, "The queen is coming home" or "Mama's baby is coming home." They knew Mom and I had secrets. We talked about things that we didn't particularly share with the others because there were certain things she only wanted me to do.

I'm my mother's executive administrator. I pay her bills and handle other types of responsibilities. In my younger years, it was so easy for us to have that type of mother/daughter relationship. Honestly, I find that I can be that way with a lot of people, as I have a knack for keeping everyone together. I'm not sure my siblings know how to do that. In spite of that small obstacle, we love each other righteously and would do anything to help one another out.

Farming was a way of life for us in Jayess, but it was a horrifying experience for me. Nothing about farm work was exciting. We rose up early in the morning, worked extremely hard all day, and repeated the same over and over, day after day. Every day we had to collect all the eggs from the henhouse and bring them inside. One day I went outside to get the eggs and saw a snake. I immediately dropped the basket and started to scream and cry while watching that snake crawl over the shells. That was the last time I ever had to collect the eggs. I was assigned a different chore. The cows needed to be milked every day, but I was afraid of them, too—especially when I had to sit on a stool, pull on their udders, and hold the milk pail steady at the same time. Nothing would come out of the udders! I could never do the job right and found it a very frustrating task. Sometimes the cows would kick my grandfather, and I always feared the same thing would happen to me.

Another one of my chores was to take water to the crew working in the field. Everyone in the household had at least one job to do. I ironed, washed clothes, and cleaned outside. Johnnie cooked for the family. When she fixed breakfast every morning, she would eat first before calling us to the kitchen. She ate as much as she wanted! The rest of us kids had to share the leftovers. I hated that because there was never enough for me and my oldest brother.

If Mom saw us just standing around doing nothing, she would say, "Go clean the outhouse." Most people these days don't know anything about having an outside toilet, which was in the outhouse. The outhouse was made of wood and had a makeshift lock on it. The fumes in that little outhouse were so bad that you'd almost choke as soon as you went inside. Ours had a tin roof that kept us dry when it rained. Rain in the South comes down hard!

My brothers, sisters, and I weren't able to start school in September like other kids. We were kept out until late November each year to pick cotton. I could pick 200 pounds when I was only 14 years old. I picked cotton throughout my childhood years. The cotton stalks were at least 8 feet tall and stretched row after row, as far as the eye could see. The whole ordeal of picking cotton was extremely intimidating.

Being afraid of everything, I would often cry when worms crawled on my cotton sack and even on my clothing and my hair. Cotton bulbs were surrounded by sharp tips that made it difficult to yank fast. Our fingertips would get pricked and bleed, making them tender and sore, but we had to keep pressing on.

When the season was over, it took three months for our fingers to fully heal, and soon the process would start all over again. Cotton-picking season was from July to November. We suffered severe back pain from bending over for 12-15 hours a day, with only a quick 15-minute break to eat and drink water. Our meals consisted of a bologna sandwich or sardines and crackers, with a soda pop. The temperature varied between 80-110 degrees, and we had to drag our own cotton sack. Because I was such a fast picker, by the end of the day, my sack weighed 200 pounds. From age 12 to 15, I accomplished this every day. That was an amazing feat for a young girl like me.

As soon as cotton-picking season was over, we were on our way to other regions of Mississippi and Louisiana to pick nuts. We gathered nuts off the ground from tung trees in designated field orchards. There were hundreds of these extremely tall trees with nuts the size of golf balls, and we carried baskets and crates to drop the nuts in. These nuts were used to make tung (also called China wood) oil.

We would get up at 3 o'clock in the morning and travel for two hours, driving to various tung oil orchard locations. These nuts were oily and left a residue on our hands. We would drag the baskets up and down the area and toss the nuts in the basket or crate, which resembled a laundry basket. Once we filled a basket, we would put it on a truck or wagon. We were paid by how many baskets we filled each day. I remember my body aching in excruciating pain from having to bend over for such long periods of time. When we were done, we had a long ride back home on the back of an open pick-up truck. Sometimes the weather was extremely cold or rainy, making the ride even more uncomfortable. If we got sick from the cold or rain, it didn't matter. We still had to go. We had work to do.

When we finally got home, it was time for bed. My oldest sister and brother and I shared a full-size bed. Johnnie and Daniel slept at the foot of the bed, and I slept in the middle, at the head of the bed. I hated this lifestyle, because going to school was very important to me. I knew education was my ticket to a better life, and I wanted to go to school so badly that I often cried. I prayed and believed that God would deliver me from the agony, pain, and suffering we endured, although I often wondered if God was punishing us as black people by subjecting us to this type of hardship.

I did this type of work until I was 18. However, I also had a job as a candy striper at a nursing home, when I was 14. This was one of my most cherished jobs, and I worked at the nursing home until I graduated from college. I got to wear a red and white uniform, and my job responsibilities entailed taking care of the elderly, very difficult and mentally ill patients, and those who could not feed themselves. I talked and read to them and helped administer their medications during the day and evening. The women loved it when I combed their hair and took them for walks up and down the hallways.

Sadly, many of them had families who had forgotten about them. Most of their families were so busy living their lives and taking care of their new families that they didn't have time to visit their elderly parents. That meant those residents also weren't able to see their grandchildren. On rare occasions, when the little ones would visit, they'd be frightened by their grandparents' physical conditions and did not want to be touched by them.

When it was time for me to leave the job for the day to attend school, my elderly friends would cry, and of course, I cried right along with them. They were my secret pen pals. I would take the time to send them notes on post cards so they could have the pleasure of receiving something special in the mail. Believe it or not, I could not wait to get back to the facility to see them when I wasn't there. Sometimes patients died before I returned to work the next day. I'd be visibly shaken after learning of their passing. These beautiful souls were my friends.

Although life at home was hard work, we had some good times, too. Thanks to our parents, we were able to have some fun and be refreshed by having some free time here and there. I remember us having a very small black-and-white television, which was about 6 or maybe 12 inches in size, and we were able to get only four stations. For many years, we wrapped a wire clothes hanger around the antenna to make the picture come in clearer. Imagine six people trying to watch that small screen at the same time. It seems comical now, but it was a luxury to us back then.

We watched TV shows called "shoot 'em ups" back then—good old westerns or cowboy flicks, like *The Rifleman* and *Gunsmoke*, because those were the ones my parents loved. Occasionally, we were allowed to watch *I Love Lucy*, *The Three Stooges*, *The Amos 'n' Andy Show*, *Leave It to Beaver*, and *American Bandstand*. During that time, *All My Children* was a hit soap opera that my mom let us watch only if our chores were done.

In the '60s, we had a projector that plugged into the TV, and my parents also had a stereo phonograph that played size 33 vinyl records! We loved listening to Duke Ellington and Mahalia Jackson. Some of my favorite artists back then were Brook Benton, who sang "It's Just a Matter of Time," and "Think Twice"; Dinah Washington, who sang "What a Difference a Day Makes" and "Unforgettable"; and Marvin Gaye; the Temptations; the Supremes; and the Four Toys.

When our parents didn't have any chores for us to do inside, we loved spending time outside playing together. We fearlessly climbed trees, even though some of us broke arms and legs and ended up walking on crutches. But that didn't stop us at all. My siblings were dare-devils, always daring each other to do something out of the ordinary.

We often played with other kids in the neighborhood after school and in the evenings after dinner. We were sent outside to play, and with the house windows open, parents could hear what their children were up to. I loved to play hopscotch, hide-and-seek, jump rope, and jacks. Like most boys, my brothers played baseball, kickball, dodgeball, and four-square. Those were some good days! We played hard and worked even harder, but when I put it all together, I learned that hard work bares great reward.

Life was really pretty simple then. We hung our clothes outside on a clothesline so the air and sun could dry them naturally. I can still remember how fresh they smelled when we pulled them off the clothesline. Sometimes, especially in the winter months, we even dried our clothes in front of the fireplace.

There's an old saying that goes, "The more things change, the more they stay the same." Just like kids today, we ate lots of junk food, like cookies with pink frosting and Stage Planks. Root beer and crème soda were my absolute favorites! We enjoyed walking to the nearby store, to hamburger stands, and to church.

In the small town of Columbia, Mississippi, we had a malt shop and cinema theatre. We could see a movie for 50 cents. There was only one bank and one women's clothing store, called Miss Poole. It was the most expensive clothing store in the area. She gave credit to all the black women who shopped there and unfairly priced items higher, which caused them to make monthly payments for many years.

At school, we had a dress code throughout the 1960s. Boys wore pants, button-down shirts or sweaters, socks, and tie shoes. No jeans, t-shirts, or sneakers were allowed outside of gym class. Girls wore skirts, blouses or sweaters, jumpers or dresses, and socks and shoes (loafers, saddle shoes, or oxfords). Clothing was primarily made of cotton or wool, no synthetics, so everything had to be ironed for school. Women wore dresses and skirts most of the time, which also needed to be ironed, as did men's clothing for work. Sheets were made of coarser cotton back then, so many sheets and pillowcases had to be ironed each week. I spent hours every week ironing.

On Christmas day, we only got one gift from Santa Claus. That was it! We girls got a doll, and the boys received G. I. Joe plastic toy soldiers. We were grateful. We couldn't conceive of the desktop computers and laptops we use now. These things didn't enter the average person's mind. We used typewriters to get things printed and to write letters to family and friends that lived far away. Email? No. Going to the post office to purchase stamps and mail letters was the only way to correspond in print.

We had one rotary telephone at home, often with a party line. You got cheaper phone service by sharing a phone line with a neighbor. Yes, that means we could listen in on one another's conversations! Frightening to think about that happening now, isn't it?

In spite of all the hard work we did during the week, we had no choice but to attend Sunday school, Bible study, BYU (Baptist Youth Fellowship), church services, revival services, and special events. Our mother believed that if she kept us engaged in biblical activities we'd be so busy that we would not have time for having sex or thinking about it. I loved reading the Bible from front to back and knew many verses from memory. I read Revelation more than any other book of the Bible. It was very frightening to read, but I wanted to know how to get to heaven and not go to hell.

One of my favorite verses is Jeremiah 29:11, *"For I know the plans I have for you," declares the LORD, 'plans to prosper you and not to harm you, plans to give you hope and a future.'"*

I attended Salem Baptist Church as a kid. Later, we attended Bethany Baptist Church in Monticello Mississippi. After moving to Foxworth, Mississippi, in the late '50s, we attended Mount Zion Baptist Church, located about 1 mile off the main road, in the woods. Someone had made a path to the church by cutting and removing thickets and branches. We only walked where grass and debris had been removed, and we had to be hyper-vigilant when it came to looking out for snakes! Just the thought of them made my flesh crawl. Many times I had nightmares and was unable to sleep. I was so afraid of everything—spiders, rats, opossums, rabbits, squirrels, armadillos, turtles, and more.

I became a Christian at an early age and was baptized in a creek by a Baptist preacher at the age of 10. I would get the Holy Ghost (Spirit) in church and shout. For you who don't know what "shouting" is, it's difficult to explain to someone who doesn't attend Pentecostal or holiness churches, but I'll do my best here. A strong, wonderful feeling of connection with God would come over me, and I'd find myself moving up and down the row I was sitting in. Sometimes I would dance or jump while also exclaiming out loud my praises to God. I would do this out of a sense of deep thankfulness and gratitude, and other times just because of the great love I had for Him. There is a scripture in the Bible that describes King David as praising God so hard that he literally danced out of his clothes. To truly understand what I am talking about, you have to experience it for yourself. I hope one day you will, because it is one of the best, inexplicable feelings I know. Believe it or not, I've never hurt myself—no aches, no pain, only praise.

I was extremely active in church. Often, I would memorize a Mother's Day message, welcome the pastor from another church, and even recite the Easter message in front of the congregation. The lady that lived next door to us was the Mother of the church. She would ask the other girls in the church, but I was the only one who volunteered to deliver her message.

While all of these activities are sometimes despised when we are young, I am so very grateful for my spiritual upbringing, because it kept me from losing my mind. It grounded me and gave me hope to believe for a brighter future when times grew dark.

CHAPTER TWO

DRIVEN BY POVERTY

The financial website 24/7 Wall St. examined socioeconomic factors in each state to determine the best and worst states to live in. The three key categories were poverty rate, education, and life expectancy. The study was inspired by the United Nations' Human Development Index. The authors noted that "life satisfaction is often based on highly subjective measures, such as whether the climate is nice, whether friends and family are present, and other factors." Mississippi had the nation's highest unemployment rate, highest poverty rate, and lowest life expectancy, making it the worst state in the U.S. to live in.[1]

A more recent study asserts that the quality of life in a particular state is largely founded on the levels of poverty, education, and health. The study noted that four key factors contributed to Mississippi's rank as the worst state in the nation: The population growth over 10 years was 6.0 percent, which is the thirteenth lowest in the country; the unemployment rate is 7.8 percent, making it the highest in the nation; the poverty rate is 21.5 percent, which is highest in the country, and life expectancy at birth is 74 years old, making it the lowest in the nation. Having the lowest median household income in the country and the highest poverty rate contributes to poorer health and, in turn, to lower life expectancy.[2]

Children who are raised in poverty are statistically less likely to finish high school. They feel they have no other choice but to help support their families and themselves by securing full-time employment. Some students who do graduate from high school may not acquire the skills and abilities needed to attain higher levels of education or to discover success in the work force at large.[3]

Our home was patriarchal. Like many families in the South, my stepfather was the breadwinner, and my mother took care of home while my siblings and I worked outside of the home. My mother and stepfather were good parents—better than good, to tell the truth. But I didn't like our environment and the condition of our home, and I didn't like growing up poor. The Bible says that God doesn't put more on us than we can bear, but honestly, there were times when I wondered if I could make it another day.

My stepfather insisted that we get an education. He knew that the best way to break the cycle of poverty was by getting a good college education. Doing so could whisk us far away from the toilsome cotton fields, dire hunger pains, and a life bound by limitations. He received no grief or pushback from me—no sir! I had a fire in me that fed my determination and resolve to make it out of the conditions we lived in. There were many times in my young life when, deep down in my soul, I felt empty and broken. I had no other choice but to escape that environment. I believed that waiting on the opposite side of that seemingly unbearable life was self-worth, high esteem, NEW direction, and peace.

I learned early that God is a God of second chances. I began to show myself new respect, stopped the negative thought patterns I had developed, and set positive goals in my mind to rehearse over and over again to prepare me for accomplishment. My stepfather planted and nurtured seeds of desire for higher learning in the soil of my heart. Education was first and foremost! My stepdad and my mother knew it was important to continually encourage my siblings and me to be the best we could be. They instilled courage and faith in us to help us face the challenges we would surely meet each day. I had learned to never give up and to try again and again, no matter how long it took to reach my goals. If my ancestors could rise above the harsh challenges handed to them through slavery, racism, and violence, I was surely going to do my best to succeed!

Many of our relatives asked my mom to give them one of her children to help our family out. Anyone visiting our home knew we were very poor and needed help. I'm certain any parent will agree that raising one child is challenging enough, but add five more, and you have a small sports team! No wonder our relatives extended their much-needed support by offering to take us into their homes. But mom's answer was always a big NO! She'd say, "We will stick together, even if we have to eat bread and drink water!"

Sadly, bread, water, and spoiled milk were the contents of our meals, pretty much every day. I hated having no choice but to eat from this limited menu, and I often refused to eat. I was a very sickly child and suffered from malnutrition because I often didn't eat much. I mean, I had to eat to live, but if I heard anyone talking negatively about food, I would not eat it. Having stomach aches, regurgitating my food, and visiting the doctor's office were regular occurrences for me. I was always taking some type of pill.

One of my biggest nightmares was having to wear my sister's clothes. I was so skinny that nothing fit me. From 8 to 10 years old, I weighed 65 pounds and ended up weighing only 98 pounds when I graduated from high school. Johnnie, on the other hand, enjoyed eating food and never had a weight issue. My mother purchased clothes particularly suited for Johnnie's size, and when Johnnie eventually outgrew them, they were handed down to me. There wasn't enough money to buy new outfits for both of us at the same time.

Figuratively speaking, Johnnie's clothes hung on me like a dish cloth. (Johnnie weighed 115 pounds.) So, yes, as you might imagine, I was completely humiliated. Think about it. What young girl do you know who doesn't desire to look pretty and attractive so she can hold her head up high with pride? I was that young girl who didn't want to stand out as different. And I was that young girl who was ashamed to wear her sister's hand-me-downs. However, with that being said, I know, if our parents had had the power to do better, they would have given us the world! In hindsight, the wisdom gained from them during those years is worth more than any money could ever buy.

Our parents provided for us the best way they knew how, and we are all very thankful for that. There was a time when my stepfather used to work out of town sometimes, doing construction on highways and buildings, to bring in income. There were no jobs in Foxworth, Mississippi, so finding work was very difficult for him. Because he had experience in building highways, he found jobs elsewhere that forced him to travel distances back and forth on a daily basis.

My parents also sold moonshine. For those of you who may not be familiar with the term, *moonshine* was any kind of alcohol, usually whiskey or rum, that was made in secret to avoid high taxes or outright bans on alcoholic drinks. The term *moonshine* originated in Britain, where it originally was a verb, *moonshining*, which referred to any job or activity that was done late at night. Poor people, black and white, sold this strain of liquor to help make ends meet. But there was stiff competition and opposition from the white community, who didn't want blacks taking money out of their pockets.

My siblings and I never made moonshine or drank any as children, but Johnnie Mae, Daniel, and I would travel outside the county and haul it back to Marion County. Once we got it back home, we would break it down, put it in mason jars or some pint bottles, and sell it. One of us was assigned to stay in front of the house and be on the look-out for the police. We had several hiding places for the liquor. We hid it in the garden, behind the chimney, inside the fireplace under the cold ashes, behind our house, and under the house, since the house was elevated off the ground. We had enough room to crawl under the house and hide ourselves. Luckily, the police didn't have search dogs back then.

One very hot and humid evening while dad was working away from home, my mother was lying on the bed resting with the windows open (we didn't have air conditioning then). Daniel just so happened to look out of the window in the nick of time to see several white police officers riding up to our house in pickup trucks. Daniel immediately alerted my mom, and she quickly passed all the whiskey she had in the bed to him. He ran outside with all the bottles as fast as his legs could carry him and crawled under the house and placed the stash at the base of the fireplace. Thank God they didn't look under the house. Heaven only knows what we might have suffered had we been found out. But, thankfully, the police left, and no arrests were made. We were exposed to liquor and cigarettes every single day, but we didn't get hooked on any of it. This deserves its own hallelujah moment!

My mother only made it to the 5th grade in school, so she could not read or write very well, but she was one smart lady! She was driven by the desire to see her children get out of poverty and lead successful lives. Mom rarely complains about anything. I learned how to be strong and to persevere in my decision making from her. I learned early that, if I had plans and goals to achieve, I couldn't focus on what things looked or felt like. I had to stay on course. I was not the typical Southern girl. I had plans for bigger things in life, and I felt that nothing, not even my race or gender or the fact that I was from Mississippi, could hinder me.

Looking back, I can honestly say that those life experiences actually gave me even more of a willingness to succeed in whatever endeavors I chose. Life as a black female in Mississippi was not easy. Most of us were groomed to be educators in the black schools or to work in some type of garment factory, making clothes. Those that were not educated found jobs in the prominent white families' homes in the area. My sights were set on moving out of Mississippi and on to a bigger scale and greater things in life.

I had always wanted to know what it felt like to have money, live in a nice home, and share the same experiences as white people. You could tell that some of them felt sorry for us, yet they never wanted to exchange places with us. The pity in their eyes was obvious, but it wasn't strong enough to compel them to help us make our lives better. And if white people did show any kindness or helped us in any way, we were told to keep it a secret because they wanted to maintain a tough attitude and avoid showing any weakness to black people. Back then, they used the forbidden word *nigger* in our faces, causing my hatred toward them to grow.

Many times, I had to remember what my mother had taught us while growing up. Her wisdom trained us to "kill them with kindness and never let anyone see us sweat." She also used to say, "You can catch more flies with honey than with vinegar," "A hard head makes a soft ass," and last, but certainly not least, "Keep talking, and I will wash your mouth out with a bar of soap."

My mother was a genius in my eyes, and she still holds that crown in my heart today. To help us keep our minds above the fray when we were growing up, she had the bright idea to order books for us to read when we had downtime. She ordered them through the mail, and they arrived every month. I couldn't wait to get my hands on them.

I believe that reading good books can build a creative, imaginative eye in all of us. I read all types of books! Comic books and mystery books about girls who used their smarts and intuition to solve the most interesting mysteries were my favorites. I also read the Bible, from cover to cover, and oh yes, Robin Hood, with his band of merry men! Then there was *Black Beauty* and many delicious romance novels about love, hate, and betrayal. Stories about handsome careless men who wined and dined naïve women, then betray them, leaving them crushed and heart-broken were also some of my favorite books to read.

My mother knew that reading these books would introduce me to new worlds, and though foreign to my young mind at the time, they might prove to intrigue and inspire me to search for something greater, outside of the walls of poverty I was encased in. It worked! My imagination was evoked, and for years my mind helped me visualize a life of possibilities that would soon become realities.

The dream of graduating from high school finally came true, followed by my exciting plan to attend college! My plan was to enroll in a four-year university and obtain a B.S. degree in business. However, during the summer break, I was involved in a serious automobile accident...a horrendous nightmare that would cast a shadow on my perfect plan.

CHAPTER THREE

KEEPING THE DREAM ALIVE

When I was 17 years old, one way I helped contribute to the family income was by babysitting and ironing clothes for white families nearly every weekend. The ironing only paid $5.00 for 8 to 10 hours of work. One particular day, a lady who frequently requested my services asked my mother if I could watch her kids so she could hang out with some of her girlfriends. Her husband was away from home in the military at the time. Usually, she would take me home when she returned from her night out, but this particular night she asked two of her male friends to take me home. I felt very uncomfortable about this but was afraid to say "no, thank you" for the ride.

Her two male friends and I left the house, got in their vehicle, and left. They sat up front, and I sat in the back. I gave them directions to my house, but they ignored me. When I repeated the directions, one of the guys said, "We want to drop something off to a guy around the corner." As they kept driving farther and farther in the opposite direction of my home, I knew something bad was about to happen.

Panic started to fill my chest, and my heart was racing. I prayed, *"Oh Lord, don't let them do what I'm thinking right now. HELP ME!"* I was a virgin, and I didn't want to lose my virginity to these two white men. I truly believed they were going to kill me. The only person who knew I was in that car was the lady that hired me to babysit, and she was cheating on her husband with these two guys. I knew she did not want that dirty little secret finding its way out in the open.

As we were riding along, the thought came to me to open the car door and jump out. We were going about 60 miles per hour, but I preferred to die rather than be raped by those men. Without thinking about it another second, I took a chance, opened the door, and jumped out onto the highway. The car swerved, and I heard the brakes make a terrible, screeching sound. Thankfully, the two men kept driving down the road. I didn't realize I was hurt until I looked down at my feet while sitting in the middle of the highway. I quickly got up off the ground, grabbed my shoes, and ran to a house across the street. I knocked on the door and started screaming, "Please help me! Please help me!"

The two men had traveled a good distance down the road, but by this time, they had turned around and started looking for me. When the owner of the house answered the door and saw me, he said, "Come in quickly!" He had witnessed the entire incident from his front window. I explained to him what happened, and he said, "I knew something bad had happened because I could hear the sound of the brakes from here." Thankfully, he got dressed and took me home.

My mother cleaned me up, and the following day she took me to the doctor and to the police station to file a report. My adrenaline had been running so high that I didn't realize exactly how hurt I was until I woke up the next morning in excruciating pain. My right ankle and one of my right toes was broken, and the skin was scraped off both my elbows. I couldn't stand on my own, so I had to use crutches to get around. Money was very tight, but my mother made sure I had the medication I needed to heal.

The police took my report, but nothing was ever done. These two men never paid for the fear and trauma their depravity caused me and my family. The entire incident was covered up. The white lady did not want to be embarrassed in the community and definitely did not want her husband to know what she'd done. When questioned by the police, she claimed she did not know the men and had just asked them to give me a ride home. This led to the question: "If you didn't know these guys, why did you have them take your babysitter home?" But again, nothing was done, and it ended there.

Mom and I discussed my going to college. She told me I might have to sit out the first semester. That news was devastating to hear. I was crushed! I immediately responded, "Oh no! I must leave for college in

September!" This was my dream, and I knew if I didn't take that first step, the delays would continue. In my experience, I have found that whenever a person proceeds to reach for his or her dreams, something or someone always show up to fight against the efforts to reach them. It never fails!

From May 15th to September 1st of 1966, I had to keep my right foot elevated on the back of a chair that was turned upside down with a pillow on it. My mother was worried that I would not be able to handle the rigors of college life in my condition, but I told her I was okay with walking around campus on crutches. In the fall of 1966, I packed my luggage, and my cousin Willie drove me to the Alcorn A&M University dormitory! Luckily, I went off to college without having to bring my crutches, and I was even able to work a part-time job in the computer department to earn extra money.

Being a brand-new freshman, I chose not to have a boyfriend because I wanted to learn how to live away from home and make my own decisions without distractions. Of course, I was tempted to reconsider my decision, but a little voice in the back of my head would always remind me, "You know what your mother told you! You don't want to disappoint her." That voice always snapped me right back in place.

In 1968, during my junior year, I worked part-time in the computer department on campus for extra spending money, and soon after, I met someone special, who eventually became my boyfriend. He had been head of the computer department for many years. He would send his secretary to get lunch for us, and we'd eat lunch in his office every day. Even though she never said anything, I don't believe his secretary liked me much. I could feel the gaze of her side-eye every time she left to pick up lunch for her boss and me. I'm sure her dislike for me had a lot to do with the fact that I was not only her boss' girlfriend, but to make matters worse, I was also her peer.

My relationship with this man grew to be very close even though he was eight years older than I. He had a daughter who was 10-years old, and he was very involved in her life. I just knew I was in love, love,

love, and felt I absolutely could not live without him. He asked me to marry him, and I could not wait for my family to meet him.

One weekend during a visit back home, I mentioned that I'd met this guy who had asked me to marry him, and I was thinking about saying YES! Without hesitation, my stepfather said, "Don't bring him here!" He then gave me a big lecture about life and how it would not be a good idea to move forward in the relationship. He reminded me that my boyfriend was eight years my senior and had a 10-year-old child. He said, "You don't know nothing about raising a child!" Since my stepfather would not welcome him into our home, we ended the relationship at the end of the school term.

As I said before, my stepfather, Lacy Hill, was an extremely loving, kind, generous, and special person. He mortgaged our home and paid my tuition for the entire four years I attended college. I worked every summer to pay the loan down. He passed away on February 10, 1999. I am ever so grateful to God for seeing fit to bring this extraordinary man into our lives. It was my honor to make him proud and have him believe that he could close his eyes satisfied with the woman I'd grown up to be.

While attending Alcorn, I also dated Willie Alexander, who played cornerback for Alcorn's football team. He was also a member of the Kappa Alpha Psi Fraternity. We dated for less than two years and broke up during my senior year. I pledged Kappa Alpha Sweetheart. My group was called SILHOUETTES. Willie later became a professional football player. He was a defensive back for the Houston Oilers for nine seasons, from 1971-1979. After his football career, he founded W. J. Alexander & Associates in 1980, an insurance brokerage firm located in Houston, Texas.

I really enjoyed college life at Alcorn. I was featured in the 1970 university book as one of Alcorn's best-dressed students on campus. I had a very old sewing machine and could whip up an outfit in two days. I was still tiny then, weighing only 115 pounds. I didn't need much fabric, so I could create a beautiful dress or blouse anytime.

My best girlfriend on campus was Gloria Hudgies. She was from Laurel, Mississippi. Her father owned Howard Corner, which consisted of a grocery store, laundry mat, dry cleaners, and a restaurant. For four years, we shared the same dorm room and had some of the best talks. She jokingly told me the only reason she was at college was to get an MRS degree. I asked her what that meant, and she explained it. She wanted to find a husband! She spent a lot of her time with a guy named Floyd, and they ended up getting married after college. Her new name (which I recently found out) is Gloria Hudgies Rice. She found me on Facebook the same day I went to a J Lo (Jennifer Lopez) concert at the Los Angeles Forum, on June 8, 2019. I will never forget. I was so ecstatic! I hadn't spoken to her since graduating from college, as we lost contact with each other. Her husband, Floyd Elliott Rice, played football at Alcorn and went on to play pro football as a linebacker for the Houston Oilers, San Diego Chargers, Oakland Raiders, and New Orleans Saints. Unfortunately, Floyd died in 2011.

During the four years, we lived together at Alcorn, Gloria and I grew to be like sisters. We shared our room with two other students; one of them was Shyan Ratcliff. Shyan was from Morton, Mississippi. She was a very sweet girl. What I remember most about Shyan is that she loved my burgundy skirt. She and I wore the same size in clothing, and at least once a week, she wanted to borrow my skirt. I hated sharing it, but I did it anyway.

My favorite snack to eat while studying was my nightly bag of Cheetos! Soon everyone in the dormitory was eating the same junk, and my snacks started disappearing. I had to lock my food up! With three roommates and people coming and going constantly, it was as if we had a revolving door, and most of the time, no one fessed up or knew who was taking my food.

Throughout college, I was able to continue working at Floridian Nursing Home as a nurse's aide during semester breaks and holidays. Mr. and Mrs. Gunn managed the nursing facility. Mrs. Gunn was a terrific boss, and she allowed me to work as many hours as I wanted, to help fund my college education. After four years, I graduated from Alcorn College with a B average.

My mom had faithfully sent me $10 a month while I was in college. I did not find out until after graduation that she had been doing this even when they did not have food in the house. I felt so bad because she had made such a great sacrifice for me. I asked her WHY? She said, "I wanted to make sure you had your own money and did not have to ask a man for money or use your body to get money." I literally cried because I was filled with gratitude. It made me love my mother even more, although my love for her was already beyond measure.

CHAPTER FOUR

I DIDN'T ASK FOR THIS

After graduating from college, I traveled to the Gulf Coast to visit Aunt Ruby. She had invited me to come and stay with her and Uncle Jessie for the summer. What a great idea! Spending time with them was always very special. I already had a job lined up in the fall in Tylertown, Mississippi, as a high school teacher and assistant to the principal, so the idea of going to a tropical coast area for the summer was an opportunity I wasn't about to miss. I'd worked hard for my college degree and was looking forward to peace and relaxation.

After staying with Aunt Ruby for two weeks, she said to me, "You're going to have to get a job." I said, "What do you mean?" She replied, "I can't afford to buy your incidentals, so you need to get a job and buy those things for yourself. You are a young lady now." I was furious! Under my breath and between pursed lips I said, "I didn't ask to come. You invited me. And now, after two weeks, you're telling me I have to find a job?" I was really upset with her.

There I was, with no other option but to begin job hunting. That very same day, I surveyed three businesses to submit applications to and called a taxi to take me to each company. I spent $32 that day on transportation alone. I submitted my first application to Ingalls Shipbuilding (now called Huntington Ingalls Industries), a leading producer of ships for the United States Navy. It is the second-largest private employer in Mississippi, right under Walmart, which is the largest. Next, I applied to work at Chevron Products Company, and third, to a chemical company that made fertilizer.

After approximately ten days, I got a call from all three companies, asking me to come in for an interview, so I did. As soon as I received word of these awesome opportunities, I called my mother and everyone I could think of to share the great news. I was so overly excited and confused at the same time, trying to decide which position I should accept. When I returned to Chevron Products Company, Mr. Hopkins, the manager of human resources, informed me of a job opening in central records and explained what it entailed. I would be pulling blueprint drawings for design engineers that came to the office looking for particular drawings. I accepted the offer and was excited to get started.

My immediate boss was a white female named Trudy. I was subjected to her daily ridicule and could feel the hostility she had toward me. She clearly thought I didn't belong there. Can you imagine being locked up in a secured room for 8 hours, 5 days a week, with a person who consistently criticized your work and constantly looked over your shoulder to see if you returned drawings to the correct location? The memory still makes me bristle at times.

As the manager of human resources, Mr. Hopkins was in charge of hiring new employees. He also conducted testing, administered salaries, etc. Mr. Hopkins informed me that another position was open at Chevron, and he wanted all female employees within the facility to take an aptitude test. I told him I really wasn't interested because I had a job waiting for me back home, and I was working there only because my aunt wanted me to. I didn't want to do this type of work all my life. But he didn't let that stop him from trying to influence me to stay. He said, "There's a laboratory position available. You don't have anything to lose."

He gathered all the women and had us take a 3-hour aptitude test. Three days later, Mr. Hopkins summoned me to his office. He said, "You know, we're looking for a female to work in the laboratory." At that time, I didn't know that there was a lack of female employees there. I had not visited the laboratory section of the company because it was so heavily secured and monitored.

He went on to say, "Well, we want to talk to you about staying. We have a job opening." I said, "I'm really not interested. I have a job, and I don't want to work in a laboratory." He invited me to do a walkthrough of the lab to see what it looked like. I agreed to go and was overwhelmed at the huge pieces of laboratory equipment. They were enormous. I'm talking about equipment that was valued at over $250,000 each. I was not going to like this at all. Memories of taking chemistry in college began to surface. In college I had worked with little Bunsen burners, thermometers, and beakers, nothing at all like what I was looking at in this billion-dollar laboratory. Again, I told Mr. Hopkins I wasn't interested, and I was adamant about it.

Here's the honest, solid truth about my determination to decline the laboratory position. At the time, I didn't want to live far from my mother. Yes, I am a mama's girl. I was purely thinking about my mother when deciding where I would choose to work. By working in Tylertown, I could hop in my car, drive about 22 miles, and make it home to my mom in the blink of an eye. That was easy.

On the other hand, I was also used to taking challenges head-on, without backing down. I can't help it; I've been that way since I entered this world. Being a dreamer and an avid goal setter remains my standard. As soon as one project is accomplished, I mark it off my list and add on a new one. Having downtime is okay, but too much downtime is a waste of time. As a kid, I spent hours alone, pondering the pros and cons of situations. Now I know that my thought processes back then were dress rehearsals for how I would perform in my future. I often asked myself, *"What's my next step?"*

After touring the lab, Mr. Hopkins brought me back to his office and said, "Well, I just want to tell you something. You aced that test!" I said, "What do you mean?" He replied, "Well, your score was 170. That is the highest score made in Chevron history on any aptitude test, ever! Before you took this test, the highest score was 70!" In that moment, he had captured my attention, and I suddenly thought to myself, *"This is music to my ears!"* Chevron was not a company that hired you without careful examination. You had to take a test so that your thought processes and test-taking skills could be evaluated

Mr. Hopkins asked me how much the teaching job at home was going to pay me. I told him I would make a little less than $18,000 a year. He then made me an extremely enticing offer that really made it difficult to turn down. He said, "Well, I'll tell you what. What if we double your salary, and you come to work for us?" That's when I started seeing dollar signs and started warming up to the idea. I told him I had majored in business education and was good at bookkeeping, short-hand, and typing. That was the type of work I'd be executing at the high school back home. I would be working both inside and outside of the classroom. That sounded great to me!

Then it began to sink in. If I accepted this position, I was about to make history. Not only would I be the first female to work as a scientist at Chevron, in 1970, but more importantly, I would be the first black woman to work as a scientist at Chevron, in 1970! This opportunity meant more than receiving a handsome salary. Could it be that God was opening a door for me to help pave the way for other black women and black men to work in prominent positions within the company, even though it would certainly attract undesirable attention and resentment? I believe this was the master plan all along, and I still remain humbled by it after all these years.

Theoretically speaking, I was familiar with being bold and taking chances. I wanted to push the envelope, as they say, and move beyond the usual, normal limits by doing something new. Chevron was taking a chance by investing thousands of dollars to equip me with knowledge, and that was an overwhelming, unbelievable, and unexpected blessing.

I guess I can't be too angry at Aunt Ruby for telling me I had to work during my first summer vacation after graduating from college. Had I packed my bags and returned home, ignoring my aunt's request, I wouldn't have experienced one of the most challenging and life-changing times of my life. Thank you, dear Aunt Ruby!

CHAPTER FIVE

FROM TURBULENCE TO A SMOOTH LANDING

If you travel by plane often, chances are you have experienced one of Mother Nature's dark moods while flying. She can show you her turbulent side and make you a Believer in one split second. Her winds can engulf a large steel flying instrument and narrow its opinion of itself down to a simple paper plane, depending on how hard her winds decide to blow. To experience her sharp attitude while moving atop her altitude is frightening, and one might just begin praying, thinking the end could be near. But having great wisdom and experience in the cockpit, and the Divine One at the helm, helps the jet resume its mid-air posture, enabling the engines to deliver its passengers safely to their destinations.

Life is that way sometimes, isn't it? Who doesn't experience metaphorical turbulence at times? We set out to journey on our paths. Everything seems fine, the views are varied and beautiful, and the rode is smooth. Then, out of the blue, something strikes us down to our knees, exposing our frailty, deficiency, and complete dependence on God.

While working at Chevron, I had such an experience. Something so devastating happened that it could have ended my life and forever closed the door to my future. Only the grace of God kept me from literally either losing my life or giving up on my dreams.

The year was 1972, and the place was Pascagoula Mississippi. I, like most young people, enjoyed going out with friends for some good, clean fun. I believed in the old saying, "All work and no play makes Jack a dull boy." A few friendly acquaintances from the Gulf Coast area invited me to go to a club one evening. So, I thought, *Why not?* The only downside to accepting the invitation from my acquaintances was that I didn't have a date to accompany me, so I wasn't excited about being the odd person out. All my buddies had boyfriends because they had lived in that town all their lives. One young lady said, "Well, I have a friend. Would you like to double-date?" I told her I wasn't really interested because I wasn't used to being with strangers, and I had never been on a blind date before. However, I told them I'd go only on the condition that the young man meet me at the club. There would be no getting into a car with someone I didn't know. No way!

We (three couples and I) went to a club called the VFW. When we arrived, I was introduced to my date for the evening, and we all started off having a great time! Later, as the evening was winding down, we all decided to walk outside to the car. The entrance of the club had excruciatingly bright lights that made it very difficult to see anything. As we were walking out of the door, someone grabbed me by my hair and literally started dragging me outside the club. I was confused and disoriented, not knowing what was going on, and I couldn't see a thing.

This person dragged me by my hair from the entrance of the club to a dark, secluded corner. When he finally released my hair, I looked up, to my surprise, to see Fred Sipp, a guy I had dated in 1970, during my summer visit with Aunt Ruby and Uncle Jessie after college. During the very short time that we had dated, he had lavished me with many gifts. He had given me his car to drive back and forth to Chevron because he didn't want me to have to get up early in the morning to take public transportation. When he got paid, he brought his paycheck straight to me. I wasn't used to taking other people's money, and I told him, "I don't want your money; I can't do that!" But he insisted! Aunt Ruby loved this guy because she loved money and had always dreamed of someone giving her nice things. I guess you could say she was living vicariously through me. Honestly, I didn't like Fred like that, but every single time he came to the house, he brought steaks, beer, or something special that my Aunt Ruby would like. "Girl, this is a good catch. I don't know any man that would willingly give you his full paycheck. You should marry him!" came ringing out of Aunt Ruby's mouth. I said,

"You've got to be kidding. He is not what I want in a man!" She spoke so highly and freely of Fred that, much to my chagrin, I stupidly agreed to go before a judge and marry him. Yes, it's true! After dating for three months, we got married and ended up getting an annulment after six months. I didn't even consider it a real marriage.

After pulling me out of the club that night, he threatened me, saying he'd rather see me dead than let me be with someone else. He had a knife, and I was staring at the biggest and sharpest blade I'd ever seen. He pointed the blade at my stomach and said, "I'm going to kill you!" He really meant it! I was scared to death, and I started praying to God. I tried explaining to him that I was just on a blind date.

I hadn't seen Fred in almost two years. I had believed that he had gone on with his life just as I had gone on with mine. I thought we had left everything fine between us. Now, I was wondering how he had found me at that club. He must have been watching me for a long time, and I had no clue. But somehow or another, he knew I was at that club that night and had come with the full intent to kill me. Thank God I was able to talk him down while my friends called the police. My blind date, James, had gone to the car to get his rifle. He was in the Air Force and had traveled from Los Angeles for training at the Keesler Air Force Base, a military base in Biloxi, Mississippi. All Air Force men had to go through that facility for training, and he kept his gun in his car. I was frantic, and thoughts were racing through my head, *Oh my God. I just met this guy, and he is going to jail for hurting Fred. His mother is going to be upset with me because she won't see her son again.*

When the police arrived, they took Fred to jail. That meant I was now on his hit list! When we were a couple, he had to be with me everywhere I went. He didn't trust anybody else talking to me or being around me, especially men. If I did something he didn't like, he would slap me or take the car keys. When he took the keys, I had to get to and from work the best way I could. I didn't have a car at the time because I'd just started working at Chevron and figured I could catch the bus. Fred worked at the Ingalls Navy shipyard and caught a ride every day with someone he knew. When I drove his car, I was allowed to drive to work and back home only. If I needed his car to go anywhere else, he had to be with me, and he would drive. In hindsight, I realize that giving me his car to drive every day, while he caught rides to work, and needing to be with me if I went anywhere other than work, should have been clear signs of his ominous and controlling nature.

Whenever Fred came to visit, my Aunt Ruby was always in the room. Everyone would be laughing and talking, so I didn't know that his dark side existed. He was an expert at hiding his extremely possessive nature, so I couldn't discern this particular character trait, and against my better judgement, I didn't slow down and take the time necessary to know him on a much deeper level.

He had the sweetest mother in the world. She was so gentle and kind, and she loved to go to swap meets in different parts of the town. She called me every so often to invite me to go with her. Fred's father was also very nice. Both of them were tickled pink that I stayed married to him as long as I did. It could have been a beautiful marriage if he hadn't been the way he was.

Although I lived in an apartment with security at the time Fred had found me at the club, I was so afraid that he would be gunning for me because he had gotten arrested that night. I knew I would be the first one on his hit-list when he got out of jail. Of course, I was right. A few days later, in the middle of the night, I heard a loud crashing sound. Someone had kicked my door down! I mean kicked the entire door all the way down with one swift kick! I had always been taught to have my house shoes and something to wear near my bed in case of emergencies. Fred had never been to my new apartment, so he didn't know where the bedroom was, thus I was able to sneak out of the side door and escape to the manager's office. The police came to my rescue and arrested him. That was arrest number two!

For a while, everywhere I went, Fred found me. I was looking over my shoulder every minute thinking, *"I have to get out of here."* I even stopped dating. It took a while to get rid of this guy. The cops talked with his parents and told them he was going to the penitentiary. After he had been arrested many times, his parents finally got serious about finding him help so he would leave me alone. Even then it was so diffi-cult to stop looking over my shoulder, thinking he would suddenly appear, so my mother sent my younger brother Michael to live with me. He stayed with me for one year, and I was so grateful.

Not long after our blind date, James and I started dating regularly. He would come to Mississippi to visit me, and I would fly to California to visit him. When James asked me to marry him, I felt I was finally going to be with a guy I could trust and who would really cherish me as his wife. The first thing he said to me after the proposal was that he was not going to live in Mississippi or anywhere else on the Gulf Coast. If we were going to marry, I would have to move to California.

Old memories from my childhood resurfaced to remind me of my dream to live in California. This was it! My dream was coming true! God was making it all happen! I was excited, and I accepted his proposal. *"But wait a minute,"* I thought. *"I can't just up and quit my job!"* I went to my manager and told him I was engaged and that my future husband lived in California; therefore, I needed to know if there were any job openings there. He agreed to check for me. It didn't take long for my manager to return with great news. There were actually three jobs available! Chevron told me they would hold all three positions for thirty days while I traveled to California to interview for them. The company also told me I could have any one of the three positions I wanted! That was sweet music to my ears and was also extraordi-narily amazing!

James formally proposed to me at my parent's house, in Colum-bia Mississippi, which is approximately a two-hour drive from the Gulf Coast. Almost as soon as we arrived, James asked my parents for their blessing, right before my mother had to scurry off to work. After receiving their blessing, he shared the good news with his mother. We had only Sunday and Monday to make it all happen because James had to get back to the Air Force Base. All of this happened on Sunday. The very next day we woke up, drove back to the Gulf Coast, applied for the marriage license, and looked for someone to marry us. I called my pastor in Moss Point and asked him to marry us. He said, "Well,

I'm about to go out of town with my fishing buddies on an exposition trip. If you don't mind me marrying you guys in my fishing boots, I'll do it!" I was so happy he said yes because I didn't know how we'd get married otherwise. I was determined to be a "Mrs." before setting foot in California!

My pastor married us and immediately left for his fishing trip. Believe it or not, old Aunt Ruby was my witness, along with my faithful brother Michael. James prepared to get back to Keesler Air Force Base before his curfew. He could not be late. He was being shipped to another location, so we wouldn't see each other for the next three to four weeks.

When James returned, we drove all the way from Mississippi to California. Saying goodbye to my mom and the rest of my family was very painful. I was used to driving to see my mother every other weekend, along with my yellow canary and my little toy poodle, named Fifi. Now we were moving over 3,000 miles away, and knowing that I would not be able to see my mom as often as I had been was absolutely heartbreaking. But I knew I was a grown woman now. I was out of college, had a job, and had gotten married. It was time for me to transition to the next phase of my life.

I cried for weeks because I couldn't see my mother. I was a big mess. My phone bills were through the roof because I called her every single day just to hear her voice. It was very hard, and I grieved a lot internally. This was a stressful time for me because I needed to make sure she was okay. This was one of the reasons why my siblings used to say that she shared things with me that she didn't share with the rest of them. My mom and I just had that type of relationship. Though I cried often and missed "my right arm," I was still very glad to be living in California. And I flew to Mississippi to see mom at least three times a year.

James and I were married for thirteen years. We have two daughters, who I sometimes believe love him more than they love me. They have an excellent relationship with their dad. Our divorce was not an amicable one, but things improved as time went on. He came to their birthday parties and other special events because I was able to set aside my personal feelings to make the girls happy. He was not abusive, but he had habits that impeded growth in our relationship. He never hit me, but he was always in competition with me.

I wanted to teach our girls values. After the divorce, they couldn't have the things they were used to getting. I felt they needed to learn how to save their allowance and work toward those Jordan sneakers they loved to wear. But James was the type that gave the most expensive gifts. The girls went to school with $150 leather book bags. He showered them with gifts. I don't know if that was to prove that he could afford it. But I was left with the bulk of the responsibility of taking care of the girls.

When James and I divorced, I told the girls to toughen up and face the facts. We had to become thrifty in our spending in order to maintain the household. But they would cry because I didn't buy them the shoes they begged for. When I told them they had to get off-brand shoes, they responded by letting me know that their daddy was going to buy them. I learned to say okay and let him do it. And he did, for four years, until he fell on hard times and could no longer afford to indulge them. The experience really showed them the truth behind what it's like to regroup and do without.

I was single for thirteen years after my divorce from James, and I was content with that. I honestly didn't care to be with anyone. I held the admiration of a few guys who desired to date me, but being brought up the way I was, I felt that, once they learned that I worked for Chevron, they saw big dollar signs. So, I always told my dates I lived in the projects right up the street and never allowed any man to come to my house. My girls were mine to protect, and I didn't want men I dated to be around them because they were so young. For thirteen years, I put my time into working at Chevron and investing in my daughters. Seven days a week, my girls were busy with piano lessons, baseball practice, cheerleading, Barbizon beauty school, Girl Scouts, and camping, and I was a Girl Scout leader for eighteen years. We went to church every single Sunday and would go out to eat afterwards, because that's the way I was brought up. We went to Wednesday night Bible study every week, too. Every day of the week we had something to do. My girls were busy, and they didn't have a choice in the matter because I was like my mama. I kept them busy to keep them out of trouble. They were involved in every activity imaginable! I put 100 percent of myself into raising my girls, and I wouldn't change a thing.

Though the girls were with me most of the time, James and I agreed to let him have them on certain weekends. Often, on the weekends he was supposed to keep them, something always seemed to come up. I believe he was trying to keep me from going out on the town or on a date. So he would become "unavailable." But I figured out a way to deal with that.

I was really trying to have a life. I went to fancy restaurants and shows or did something spectacular with whomever I was dating at the time, and I didn't have to worry about the girls. But when my dates would bring up the "M" word, I would let them know that I wasn't there to marry anyone. My mom's wisdom and warnings stuck with me. And she always taught me to have my own money whenever I went on a date. I always let my dates know upfront that I could afford to pay for my own meal. If they did pay for my meal, they did it of their own free will. I was not going to share my body with any of them.

In the 1980s and 1990s, if men spent over a certain amount of money on women, they expected to be compensated by having sex with them, which in my opinion, is equal to prostitution. I often told men that I didn't handle myself in that fashion. Some guys were happy I was very frank with them. Others still tried to cross my boundaries, even when I told them I would not be changing my mind. I always drove my own car and told them to meet me at the restaurant or wherever we were going because they could not come to my house. I hired some-one to come in and take care of the girls and spent a lot of money to make sure they were protected because I never forgot that night, when I was seventeen.

Then Mr. Bennie Harris, Jr. enters the scene, stage right! I really believe God sent him to me. I prayed every day for God to send me someone. Looks were not a priority for me. I wanted someone who would be good to me and not be physically abusive. I knew if some-one tried to lay their hands on me I would go to jail because I didn't play that at all. If I didn't like getting whelps on my skin from getting spankings as a child, do you really think I wanted to bear the angry marks from being slapped around by a grown man? Absolutely not!

I prayed for a good man, someone who loved God, loved going to church, and would be a good stepfather to my girls. Then there was this gentleman that I would see in the grocery store and at church from time to time. Every time our eyes met, he would give me that little extra look, and I thought *Oh, okay.* I thought about how interest-ing he seemed, and he wasn't bad on the eyes either. He was actually quite handsome.

One day, we ran into each other at the grocery store, and we started talking. He told me he was a divorcee as well. That was certainly a plus. He asked me to go out with him, so we started to hang out a bit. I told him I wasn't looking for anything serious because I didn't want him to think I was really looking for a husband. The truth, of course, was that I really wanted to be married, but I didn't want him to think I was after him. I don't like guys thinking that I'm chasing them, so when we started dating, I told him we'd just take it a day at a time, with no strings attached.

Several months later, Bennie said, "Well, I think we should go steady." We started going out more and did some amazing things together. We went to Paris, Niagara Falls, Maui, Martha's Vineyard, and Australia and stayed in fancy hotels and lived life in a way I had dreamed of for years. Traveling was always something I wanted to do. I had bought a timeshare back in the '80s. Every year my girls and I went somewhere different: The Bahamas, Hawaii, New York, and many other wonderful places.

One day I told Bennie we were going to Paris, so we packed our bags and flew to one of the most romantic destinations in the world. I remember wanting some ice cream one day, so we walked into McDon-ald's and got some ice cream and sat on some stools to eat it. The next thing I knew, Bennie had popped the big question. He asked me to marry him right there while I was sitting on that stool. I almost fell off of it! I was hoping he would ask me someday. He had been making these special plans for a while and had already talked to my girls to let them know he wanted to be my husband. Although my girls liked Ben a lot, they were very close to me, and because they had had me all to themselves for so long, they really didn't want me to get married.

Not long after Ben had talked to the girls about proposing marriage, they brought up the conversation while I was driving them to an event one day. My daughter Shanta said, "Mom, are you really going to marry him and leave us?" I pulled over to the side of the highway and stopped the car. I said, "Look! Whether you approve or not, I am marrying this man because he's nice, and he's a good person. You guys have been around him long enough to know that he's a good man." They agreed with me and decided to let their guards down and accept the fact that they would be inheriting a wonderful stepdad.

When we returned from Paris, I began to plan the perfect wedding. I must have spent $40,000. Almost twenty-five years ago, our spectacular outdoor wedding was held at the beautiful Chevron Park Clubhouse, in El Segundo, California. I wanted everything to be perfect. I even rented an old vintage car that looked like it came straight out of the 1940s. We had four pastors officiate in different capacities.

Sometimes I still pinch myself because I'm really feisty, and I want everything. I'm always all over the place doing things, and my wonderful husband keeps me grounded. Ben goes out of his way to make me happy and keep me satisfied. He even does the little things that mean a lot. My girlfriends noticed his qualities immediately. They've told me I am so lucky to have such a good man. Ben is right beside me at every event I'm involved in. I drag him everywhere, and he never complains. He works hard to make sure everything runs smoothly. I'm so very blessed to have him in my life!

CHAPTER SIX

170! THE HIGHEST SCORE EVER!

Yes, I really did score 170 on the aptitude test at Chevron, and it was the highest score anyone had ever made on the exam. It's true! No one else, male or female, black or white, had ever scored so high on Chevron's aptitude test. Either I was that smart or God gave me the answers on that test because He had a purpose for me as an employee at Chevron. You may be saying, "But, Alene, you were always a scaredy-cat! How could you accept a position that you already knew had the potential to take you through hell?" My answer to you is this. I had a relationship with God, and I prayed a lot. I knew when He was leading me, and I had a gut feeling that Chevron was the place where He desired me to be. Sometimes we just have to trust our instincts and lean on the discernment God places on the inside of us that acts as a compass and guide. Plus, that was an amazing salary for a young black woman like me. Choosing not to accept the position would have been foolish.

I started working for Chevron as a scientist on October 1, 1970. Believe it or not, after I accepted the position, I asked myself, "What did I just get myself into?" I had taken two semesters of chemistry in college, and I knew how to operate in a small classroom setting, where I had learned how to take the temperature of products. But that was nothing compared to what I witnessed the first time I walked into that laboratory at Chevron. There were thousands of equipment pieces, all different types, lines, and sizes, not to mention the wires and alarms. Feeling overwhelmed is an understatement. As I stood there on my first day, I said "God, help me!"

The lab was massive and housed huge equipment everywhere! Some pieces even had hoods over them. There were heating baths.

Some were round and filled with oil, and tubes ran throughout them. It was difficult for me to process it all. But despite the tremendous fear I had, I made up my mind to try. God was going to help me get through it. Being fresh out of college, I didn't have a problem learning things. I knew the order of the processes and how to write reports, and I understood the time elements involved. I was driven!

Chevron had a formal job qualification program that included basic training, refresher training, and job qualification tests. Fully trained inspectors and technicians were knowledgeable in, but not limited to, measurement technique, analysis technique, product characteristics, problem-solving, and testing variation. Laboratory technicians were trained in the requirements of ASTM methods they performed, including assurance that the test results they produced were technically sound and defensible. I was so relieved and comfortable knowing that Chevron had a detailed outlined program with precaution and accuracy guidelines in place for my safety and the safety of others. All new technicians were trained on each test method individually, under management supervision. After the technician had demonstrated competence with and accuracy of a test method, the lab manager or supervisor would authorize and approve the employee to conduct that test method without supervision.

There were six of us in the program. We were given reading material from the ASTM Procedure Book. This book governed how we performed in testing. It showed us exactly what to do. The instructors would lay everything out on a table and say, "You need this type of chemical. You need this type of syringe." They showed us all the different tools necessary. They then showed us how to test different samples and use chemicals. We were told that we had to focus intently, using precision to arrive at the precise final results necessary. Guidelines had to be followed exactly. There were no shortcuts. Outcomes would reveal the truth if we had tried to abbreviate the process.

Once the instructor demonstrated how to do the test from start to finish, he'd leave you alone in the room to practice what he'd just taught. The following day, a test would be given on what had been taught the previous two days, and if you did not make a score of at least 70 on the detailed questions that were asked after three of four times, you were not considered to be progressing. Strict records of our progress were kept. If the instructors found that we couldn't keep up, then, to them, we weren't showing potential, and were dropped from the program.

There were only two of us left in the program when I graduated. The others were not able to keep up because they didn't harness the necessary discipline to get in there, listen, and perform the tests. We were paid to learn how to run the tests. If you stayed in the program and did well, you received a raise every six months. After being there a year, you'd get another raise and a new title. Then, during the second, third, and fourth years, you worked to become a fully qualified lab technician.

The tests we had to run were difficult and tedious. I recall one where you had to run a flash test. To determine the flash point, you had to follow the rules exactly. A specific instrument had to be used to acquire a precisely accurate test result, and it had to be done manually. You had to put your head over the instrument and look into a tiny little cup. You also had to be extremely careful because oil could blow back in your face, or a fire could start. All of this had to be done with complete accuracy, with only seconds to spare.

When I retired from Chevron, I was given some of the equipment as mementos. One of the mementos I have is a physical flash machine that I used in the laboratory. I kept it because the tests I ran using that machine were highly intimidating. I conquered my fear of that piece of equipment, and I wanted to keep it as a reminder that nothing is too difficult if you persist. Anything is possible!

When conducting the flash test, you had to put your head under a hood and keep doing it for a few seconds until it flashed. That's why it's called a flash test. Flash tests are necessary to make sure fuel temperatures are correct before the fuel is released to travel across country, or anywhere else, for that matter. Let's use diesel fuel as an example. The diesel had to remain at a certain temperature so the trucks that ran on diesel wouldn't blow up. There were certain specifications that had to be met. Otherwise, production would be ruined or stopped completely, and Chevron could possibly be sued.

Chevron ran jet fuel through an underground pipeline to LAX to fill up the jumbo jets used by commercial airlines, so testing was very stringent. Everything we did had a specific testing guideline. No one was ever placed in a testing section they did not know. If an off test of jet fuel was released, an aircraft's engine could be affected while in the air, or an explosion could occur. But thank God we had well-trained employees who took safety and testing seriously. If a small aircraft is issued an incorrect grade of fuel, the engine could very likely incur severe damage, and lives could be lost. All Chevron products can be traced to the company that procured them. Therefore, quality had to be maintained at all times. If not, lawsuits would be imminent.

I was the Chevron ISO 9001Coordinator at the El Segundo Plant. My assignment was to get the Distribution Lubricants Center certified. ISO 9001 is an internationally recognized quality management standard that specifies requirements for a quality management system that must be met by companies to fulfill customer expectations and requirements for products and services. When applied, this standard should support companies in becoming more efficient and increasing customer satisfaction.

Some of my favorite testings that I learned and had to run quite frequently throughout my career at Chevron were:

- ✿ aviation fuel used in small aircrafts
- ✿ jet fuel used by commercial airlines
- ✿ gasolines: various grades used in cars
- ✿ diesel fuel: The submarine ships used diesel fuel to run their generators which provide power to charge their batteries – U.S. Navy contracts
- ✿ traveling to other Chevron facilities to troubleshoot equipment and to train other employees or receive refresher training for myself to keep abreast of new changes or guidelines for testing
- ✿ kerosene– used for cooking, heating, and lighting
- ✿ motor oils and transmission fluid for vehicles

Thinner products were my least favorite tests because of the hazard components.

I really did enjoy my job, but the tension the human body takes on in this position is tremendous. It was extremely stressful work. The stress alone could cause you to lose your job. Every test we performed had our personal signature on it. So, management knew who was responsible—good or bad. There were two physical areas that were characterized as the Light Side or the Dark Side, and a supervisor would let you know each day which side you were assigned to. The light side of the laboratory handled aviation gasolines and thinner products, which are used to make paint. These are considered light products. Then you might be assigned to the dark side, which handled jet fuel, diesel, and crude oils—dark products.

Wherever you were assigned, you had to be ready to handle the tasks at hand. You had to continue to study the ASTM books, study your procedures, and be alert at all times. There was no fooling around in the laboratory, nor could you come in sleepy or distracted. You had not only your own life to protect but also the lives of others. The lab is set up with so many chemicals and combustible products that could potentially cause massive fires. This career is to be taken very seriously. Like a surgeon performing heart surgery, there must be precision, precision, precision!

This was the type of work I did for many years, and some of the work was more detailed than I have explained here. I earned a reputation of being trustworthy. I had trained vigorously and had college experience undergirding me, so believed I could do it. I also had something to prove to myself and others, being that I was a product of affirmative action in the '70s, when businesses were under mandates to hire females and African Americans. I felt I owed it to myself and to future young, black women coming behind me who desired to work in laboratories and take on responsibilities like mine to be the best I could possibly be.

Sometimes, when I think about the awesomeness of it all, I pinch myself. I was a young, black woman left all by herself, in a high-functioning laboratory, signing and approving multibillion-dollar contracts, and I was asked, "Okay, based on your results, what do you say?" Whatever answer I gave was what they went with. News spread about me around Chevron quickly. I remember one particular night shift, at approximately 1:00 a.m., when the plant manager needed a special test run on a simulated engine in the engine room located outside of the lab inside of an isolated area. I was asked to try running a test to get a quality control result. I had been trained on this test several times, so I grabbed my training notes and attempted to perform the test using gasoline inside of the engine. The results were perfect, and the manager was able to release the product to the Blending & Shipping Division. The trucks that had been waiting within the refinery for the results could finally be filled up by a trained certified operator. Since then, every time they needed that test run in an emergency situation, if I was working that particular shift, I was the person designated to do it. If there was an issue with a laboratory test, I was the first go-to person.

After working as a lab technician, I became the trainer of new employees entering the laboratory. Chevron gave me my own office. Videotapes were produced to show incoming lab technicians how to run the various tests, and I no longer had to work rotating shifts. I had a strictly day job. Upper management left the responsibilities in my hands, and I passed down the same processes the company had taught me when I first began working in the department. New lab techs were tested every two days, and they had to make a certain grade and perform specific tests. Upper management liked to say that new managers change with time and that I took a little too much time training new employees. They wanted to get the new employees into production quickly, so I was always fighting back, trying to get them to understand that the time I took for training the new employees was necessary. We had to make sure people were trained properly so there would be no laboratory incidents. I was always pushing back, but I got the job done. My self-esteem and confidence were high. If you gave me a job to do, then I would always do my best. It may have taken me a little bit longer, but I always completed the task on time.

I soon move up to the head inspector and had to review and inspect everyone's work in the laboratory, on both light and dark sides. I also released product to operations so they could fill up trucks going to the airport. In addition to the underground pipeline, we also had trucks that came to pick up finished products. Have you ever noticed those signs on the back of huge trucks warning drivers that they are hauling a type of product that is highly flammable? When I'm on the highway, I always give these truck drivers respect. They are carrying a huge responsibility.

When I first started working in the lab, the men weren't very helpful at all. So, I knew from the start that I was on my own. These men resented me because they had lost some of their privileges. There was no restroom for women at the time because the men were using that space as a break room to take naps or to do whatever else they wanted. After I started working there, a door sign had to be placed on the door, saying "Women Only."

Oftentimes, when I needed to run various tests, I couldn't find the necessary supplies. Some of the men were devious, and they hid them or placed obstacles in my way so that I would have to spend time searching for them. These tests were time-sensitive, and I often only had minutes, sometimes mere seconds, to complete them. The resentment was strong. The hatred was palpable. Some of these men didn't really understand affirmative action. They felt that "this black woman is in our way, and we don't want her here." I had to be extra careful and friendly to protect myself and keep the peace, even down to putting food in the refrigerator. I had already heard that one guy had a habit of eating everyone's food, so fellow employees would put laxatives in the food to make him sick. So, I had to be very careful to keep all my things together under my desk or in a locker.

I chose to be humble and portray an image of someone eager to learn. In time, some of them came around and started being helpful. But when I started moving up the ranks, the resentment returned because they felt I was being given certain privileges that I, as a black woman, shouldn't have had. Some of them actually said, "Well, I've been here all these years, and this never happened to me!" So, I had to watch myself at all times.

I remember a test result of mine not coming out right once because someone had tampered with it. I had to start all over again and redo the test as upper management waited for me to finish. If a product needs to be released to the refinery, for instance crude oil, and it needs to have ten different tests completed, everything on each test has to be done within a minimum and maximum specification. If nine tests were run and the tenth test is not correct, the product cannot be released for sale to anyone. Now, in this case, upper management was upset and frustrated because the samples I was testing had been in the laboratory for two days and were not ready. Then the refinery manager was calling, his boss was calling, and a driver was outside sitting in a truck and had been waiting all night for the product to be tested. A decision had to be made, but I wasn't going to be the one to release a test if it did not meet the specification. I would not sign my name on the dotted line. The best thing for me to do at that point was to start over. There were times when the trucks had to wait an additional two to three hours before a product was released. That meant the company was losing money, and the product recipient waiting for its arrival was losing money, too. I had been sabotaged. But success was still in my corner, as I would redo the test and come out with a good number so that I could release the product

This type of pressure was bad for me internally, but my pride would not let me pencil in false numbers and release something incorrect. A sample of every product that is released must be kept in a protected area. Each sample must be labeled with the lab technician's name, along with the time of day it was released. For up to one year, these samples can be sent to various laboratories outside of Chevron to determine if it is correct or incorrect. I was usually involved with getting the end result, making decisions, and presenting the information to the manager. The pressure was high, and I daily committed to following guidelines. Employees were fired for giving erroneous information, which often caused the company to suffer many lawsuits.

I made sure I checked and could stand behind everything I did, and I am grateful to God that, in all my thirty-eight years at Chevron, I never had a major incident, never had any contamination of products, and never released anything that was off test. When training new employees, I would always share the pros and cons. Mainly, I'd let them know that they could not hide anything and they should speak out if something is wrong.

The stress kept me at the doctor's office for anxiety pill prescriptions. The pressure I felt kept me from being able to relax. I was always having to watch my back, and I was constantly thinking about being away from my family. Before I started working only day shifts, working rotating shifts was like living in a perpetual nightmare. There were so many times when I wanted to quit, give up, and just throw my hands up and say it wasn't worth it. I did a lot of praying. And although my faith in God is strong, I had to go to the doctor and take pills because my anxiety felt unmanageable. I could never relax. Working in a laboratory is working with the unknown, trying to find the solution. I cried often. I would go in the restroom and cry, but when I came out, no one ever knew I'd shed a tear. My mom always said, "Never let them see you sweat. You just have to go to the car or the bathroom and be a baby and cry it out. Then suck it up and get back to work." I portrayed a composed image at Chevron at all times. I'd constantly remind myself: "You're the only black woman in the laboratory, and everyone hates you because they feel this is a man's world." In their minds, I was there only because they had to hire me. But I knew better.

My first daughter, Nakita, was born on March 18, 1976. I was working in the refinery laboratory during that time. I discovered that there were no guidelines in place at Chevron for pregnancy or maternity leave at that time. Nothing. So, when I disclosed to them that I was pregnant, everyone was in a tailspin because there were also no guidelines in place to protect a growing fetus from being exposed to the harsh chemicals I worked with every day.

I worked with acids, Benzene, Toluene, and all different kinds of chemicals that required a mask to be worn. If instructions said to wear gloves, I wore gloves! If they said wear a mask, I wore a mask! The ventilation in the laboratory was poor. I was exposed to all sorts of dangerous substances that I should not have been around while pregnant. Every single Chevron facility was contacted to see if there were any written policies in place. Nothing. They scurried to write guidelines. I was just grateful I had a normal childbirth, and my beautiful baby was born with no birth defects. Now, Chevron and their female employees are protected because of policies and procedures that were put in place back then, for me and my growing family.

In 2008 I decided to take an early retirement from Chevron's El Segundo facility. I'd worked there for thirty-eight years and three months. I was really trying to go for forty years but decided against it. Money is not everything, and by the grace of God, I'd made it through without any major incidences. When I left, Chevron had to outsource a lot of their testing to another lab. I had created a desk manual for every test we ran. It was an A to Z procedure book that showed how to run every test, but no one desired to fill my position as laboratory supervisor. I'd made it look easy all those years, but when the procedures were shared, no one wanted the job. In 2008, The El Segundo Distribution Center laboratory was downgraded to a satellite office because no one wanted the tremendous responsibility that came with overseeing it.

This lubrication division was the second department I worked in, and it dealt with various grades of oils for cars, such as Delo 400 30, Delo 400-15/40, transmission fluids, hydraulic fluids for heavy equipment, etc. I ordered all the supplies necessary for testing, made sure employees were there on time, made sure all equipment in the laboratory maintained a calibration (a very lengthy and tedious process), changed the tubing for the equipment to maintain accurate test results, and made sure all paperwork and payroll was done and that employees received their paychecks.

One of my scary job responsibilities was being a "firefighter." Whenever there was a fire in the refinery, preassigned employees had to suit up in their fire gear, hop on the back of the fire truck with other employees, and go fight the fire within the refinery. I frowned on that requirement because I was not a trained firefighter.

ADMINISTRATIVE CONTROLS LABORATORY AUDIT TEAM

Formal records were maintained for measurement data, analytical data, equipment calibration, equipment maintenance, equipment repair, and employee records that pertained to job qualifications (i.e., licenses, training, work experiences, education, etc.). Documented practices exist for sample and data integrity.

I was promoted to laboratory supervisor in 1982 and worked in that position for twenty-six years, and during that time, other special assignments were added to my responsibilities. As a laboratory supervisor, another one of my job responsibilities was to document a SOP (Standard Operating Procedures) manual, which is a written step-by-step instruction guide compiled to help workers carry out complex routine operations. It had to be readily available to employees and be appropriately maintained. A formal quality control manual, specific to the site, must exist that explains laboratory and control measures. The laboratory control samples (LCS's) and statistical control charting are used by the analyst to ensure technically sound data. These samples are placed in a retain room, are carefully identifiable, and MUST be found when needed for auditing purposes. I had to make sure employees received safety and quality control training, since our lives and the lives of other employees and the surrounding communities, as well as the refinery plant, were at stake. I had to make sure all contracts signed by me had Chevron's best interest at heart. They were scrutinized very carefully.

I also was involved in hiring and firing employees from Chevron and administering employee PMP reviews. The PMP process entailed a documented professional appraisal and a regular review of an employee's job performance and overall contribution to the company. It also evaluated an employee's skills, achievements, and growth or lack thereof. Whenever lawsuits were brought against Chevron in my division, I had to represent Chevron in court before the judge.

I was also part of Chevron's internal and external audit team. We were a group of employees from various Chevron facilities who would fly into chosen facilities and observe Chevron personnel actually running test methods while others observed the process. A person was selected who actually ran tests on a daily basis as documented in sample logs. Randomly, a gasoline, jet, diesel, gas, oil, or some other type of sample was selected. This procedure took approximately four hours, from start to finish.

RETIREMENT

At Chevron, employees are rewarded and celebrated for every ten years of service. For the first ten years, they receive a diamond inlaid pen. We always went to high-end restaurants and invited all our family members, along with a few close friends, when we celebrated. I chose Yamashiro as the restaurant for my retirement party, and I ordered whatever I wanted on the menu! Steak and lobster were my choices, but no one was surprised because I always ordered the best! And besides, after all I had been through, a decent meal wasn't too much to ask for.

It was a happy time and a sad time. I had made the decision to finally enjoy my life and get away from the chemicals. But this was around the time that Chevron had a buyout. They were giving employees the opportunity to choose to stay or take a year's salary and move on. If employees decided to stay, there was the uncertainty of having to transfer out of state. There were several options on the table. What did I want to do? Should I retire, take the year's salary, or remain and take the chance of being transferred to Texas, South Carolina, or even Russia? I decided to stay in California and take the early retirement. I could have stayed another ten years, made great money, and earned a larger retirement distribution. Bottom line, I left while I didn't have any major health issues, and I don't regret my decision at all.

Leaving Chevron didn't mean I couldn't be a viable force elsewhere. Community activism is now my wheelhouse and takes me all over the country. I am dedicated to helping people overcome obstacles, large or small, that can keep them from reaching their goals and highest potential. After all, if I endured and overcame the difficulties thrown onto my path, so can others. I am driven to share my story. As a songwriter wrote in a well-known spiritual hymn, "If I can help somebody as I pass along, then my living will not be in vain."

CHAPTER SEVEN

FROM SCIENTIST TO COMMUNITY ACTIVIST

It was unbelievable. I could not believe that I had stayed at Chevron for thirty-eight years. After retirement, I was completely lost, yet I was rejuvenated and excited, knowing I didn't have to get up at 4:30 a.m. ever again unless I really wanted to. Before retirement, I had gotten up every morning at 4:30 a.m. The first thing I did was work out for a half-hour. Then I'd take a hot shower, get dressed, and go to work. It was important that I be in the office at 6:00 a.m. on the dot. Back then, pollution was very heavy, and sometimes visibility was so poor you could hardly see the car in front of you. So, I'd give myself an hour and a half to get to the office.

Retiring was a dream come true, and I think I literally cried because I never thought I'd last that long. Thirty-eight years and three months. My career as a Chevron employee lasted from October 1, 1970, to December 1, 2008. I honestly felt it was time. Some of my friends had worked up to and past full retirement age, and when they finally retired, they had health issues and could not enjoy life as they had hoped and planned. I did not want that to be my experience.

I was experiencing feelings I'd never felt before. I thought about how difficult it had been to reach that point without giving up and staying the course. That was the biggest thing: staying the course. There were so many times I wanted to quit because of the things I'd faced. When I transferred from the Chevron Refinery Laboratory to the Chevron El Segundo Lubricant Division, I discovered that it was a training camp for white males, where they could learn how to manage a division.

These men stayed for two years and were then able to transfer and get their own distribution facility or move into a higher position.

Some of the men who came through were so mean—just difficult! And there I was, with twenty-five years of service, with no black mark on my record, ever, and yet there was one particular man who made it so difficult that I had to go outside of the distribution center and talk to his manager. This man had no experience in laboratory work, processes, or procedures—nothing, no experience! He talked a good game. He was very articulate, and he wanted to impress. There were many times when he wanted to write me up, saying that I didn't do this or that. So, I had to fight him. I had to beat him at his own game.

A few times he said things to me privately that were laced with prejudice. I just made my plans and said to myself "Okay. You will go before I will!" I felt working for twenty-five years meant something with the company, so I started documenting things on him. There were times when he left work early, and since I had keys to all the offices, I used to look through his trash can after he'd gone to find pertinent and confidential information I could use. I discovered an incriminating document on which he'd made some derogatory statements about black people. I shared that piece of information with his boss. The company let him go without completing his training. He went back to Michigan to run his father's furniture store.

I had to take action. I later found out that he had been going through my files and getting information, but he didn't really understand the ramifications of testing anything. Therefore, going through my files proved to be fruitless. It takes a long time to learn the chemical process of getting an analysis. He thought stealing information from my files and talking to my superiors would be effective. But he was wrong.

Almost every two and a half years, for twenty years, a new manager was brought to the lubricant refinery. Each one would try to set new boundaries, rules, and regulations. Some were very good, and some were terrible. Dennis Ofcadek stayed three years, and we hated to see him go. He was our manager during the time when Chevron was downsizing. They felt my division had too many employees, yet I held four or five different positions. I was the lab supervisor, OCS analyst, policy 530 coordinator, and payroll supervisor, and I filled in for the plant manager whenever he had to leave for training or was on vacation. I ran the facility myself and made major decisions. I had to make sure all the employees got paid and that we received all our raw materials, whether they came in on ships, barges, or trucks. We got a lot of blending components from different foreign companies located in various places, such as Russia and parts of Africa. Samples of material had to be taken by plant operators and brought to the laboratory for testing, so the ships had to be docked until we finished a series of testings.

Instead of having one operating control analyst position, there were two. There was a secure room built within the office building, and only I and another coworker could enter the room. A special phone was installed in my home so I could be on call at night. My job was to make sure that everything was tested and that everything coming onto the plant was documented on a reel. It had to be backed up. The machines in the secured office recorded every single activity each day. If anything happened during the recording process while I was away, for instance, if the equipment ran out of tape or an alarm went off, I would be called at home and have to get up, go to the refinery, and handle the problem. Making certain we had the data and that it was retained was critical. I made on-call trips back to the job many, many times.

Every department experienced mandatory down-sizing. During this period, Dennis had to decide whether I or the other operating analyst would remain at Chevron El Segundo. There were openings in Texas. That meant we could keep our job if we were chosen to relocate. We weren't given a choice; we had to pack up and go if we wanted to remain employed by the company. One day, Dennis gathered all of us into a room and began calling out names. He said something like "John Doe, you no longer have a job here at El Segundo. You are being transferred to (*wherever the location was*)." When my position came up, my coworker was told that he had to take the job in Texas, so I was able to stay in El Segundo. I was relieved. The only thing I didn't like about the way Dennis handled this situation is that he had been aware of this change for three weeks. He could have called each employee into his office soon after he was aware of the need to relocate certain employees and broken the news to them privately. My coworker was furious and didn't speak to me for three weeks. Tensions were high, and there was great division among employees. Everyone at the facility knew who was staying and who wasn't, and it created a really bad atmosphere.

Dennis was the best manager I ever had. Whenever outside managers came to visit the refinery and meet with Dennis, I would pick them up from the airport. I had a company car to drive, which made the task much easier. Whenever these visits occurred, Dennis would always ask me, "Where are we going for lunch?" I loved trying new restaurants. Whenever we celebrated employee milestones, I chose the location of the celebration. One of my favorite places was Johnny Rebs' True South, in Long Beach, because they serve scrumptious Southern dishes. For Dennis' birthday, I called ahead to let them know it was my boss' birthday, and oh man, I thought I was going to get fired. The wait staff made Dennis stand up in the restaurant, dance, crush peanut shells on the floor, and wear an ugly cowboy hat. For another part of the birthday ritual, he had to kiss a pig statue's rear end. Dennis was visibly upset. He rolled his eyes and turned beet red, but he got over it. Every time we had higher-ups in the company visit El Segundo, we always went to Johnny Rebs,' and the experience became a running joke. Dennis would give them the experience I had given to him.

Believe it or not, my first few days and weeks of retirement were spent thinking about all those things. Thirty-eight years is a very long time. My life was tied to Chevron, and allowing myself to let go took some time. I didn't know what to do with myself during my first few days of retirement. I often reminisced, thinking about everything—what God had brought me through, because, to me, the things that I did were out of the ordinary. I also knew I'd be missed.

For a while, I didn't really rest. I'm used to getting into things. I thought about what I was going to do after retiring while I was still working at Chevron. I set goals for six to eight months. Then I started studying at night and earned my real-estate license and started selling houses. I sold houses for twelve years. I also got my notary public license and became a mobile notary. These two certificates were important to me. I wasn't going to sit around the house and do nothing. As soon as I retired, my managers asked me what I was going to do, and I told them I was already a real estate agent and a notary, and they couldn't believe it.

Anything that you did to make extra money while working at Chevron had to be kept to yourself because, when the time came to get a raise, management would try to take money from you. I never felt quite comfortable as a black person sharing my personal business with anyone. I even used to park my Mercedes Benz far away from the refinery so they wouldn't see. I knew it would have been an issue. If they had seen me driving a car like that, they would have felt that they were giving me too much money. The day I knew I was retiring, I drove up in my Mercedes and stepped out right in front of my boss. He exclaimed, "Where did you get that car from?" I said, "Man, I've had this for two or three years!" "...What?" he said, with his mouth wide open. And yes, it was clean and shiny! Hey, I was retiring, so I started showing my hand. I showed them what I had accomplished over the years but could never share with them while I was working there. They were always bragging about how they got new houses and bought different stocks, and of course, I would listen. But I never told them what I had because I knew when I left I wanted to be comfortable, and I didn't want them messing with my money. It's really sad that it had to be that way, though. I'll never forget the look on my boss' face when he saw me step out of my Mercedes!

There is a season for everything. Verses in the book of Ecclesiastes tell us so. My season as a scientist had ended, and soon after, my new career in real estate began. I started working part-time for Century 21 in Hawthorne, California. I went to the office, sold houses, and really enjoyed my new field. But as time went on, my husband started to complain that I was gone all the time. He wasn't lying. I was in Palos Verdes and different places holding open houses, and he felt that I was away too often. After twelve years, I stopped selling real estate. If Ben wanted me with him, I couldn't do both.

My attention then turned to various other activities, and I decided to run for city council in 2013. Running for office is an expensive and cruel business, but I won't go too far into explaining that part of it. I later ran for Carson City Treasurer against a woman who had been in the position for years. I didn't win, but I learned a lot from the experience. I became more active in the community and was a Commissioner for many years. I was chairperson for the Parks and Recreation Commission and was on the Carson Citywide Commission and various other commissions. I became interested in philanthropy and began holding fundraisers. I was nominated Woman of the Year by Assemblyman Isadore Hall, from the 35th district, and Assemblyman Warren Furutani, from the 55th district. I received the Franklin Delano Roosevelt award in 2010, and was a 2008 delegate for the Democratic Party during Barack Obama's bid for the presidency. I also traveled to the DNC Convention in 2009.

I got to know Governors Jerry Brown and Arnold Schwarzenegger, and Arnold's wife, Maria Shriver, who held her yearly women's conference at the Long Beach Convention Center. I worked as a volunteer with her for four years. I also recruited kids to get involved in breast cancer walks within our communities. I worked with the Girl Scouts for eighteen years, taking them all the way to the top under George W. Bush's presidency. Every now and then I run into some of the girls, and they still recognize me. As grown young women, they share how grateful they are for the time we spent together. Sometimes, as you get older, you can forget all the things you've done. Being reminded that I was able to help someone makes me feel empowered to do more.

I am currently chairperson of the National Congress of Black Women Los Angeles Chapter. I started with them in 2009 as chaplain, then worked as their financial secretary, then treasurer, then first vice president, and now chairperson, until 2021. Each year I have received the "Angel Award" from the CEO/president of NCBW, Dr. E. Faye Williams, at their annual brunch, in Washington, D.C.

I had the awesome opportunity to meet Shirley Chisholm, the founder of NCBW, when she visited Alcorn's college campus in 1969. She enlightened us by informing us that black women and families were the most underserved population in our country. Her passion to help them move out of that statistic ignited something in me, and I've held on to that flame ever since. Twenty-five years later, I am honored to represent this organization as chairperson. Taking on this position was a very proud, full-circle moment for me. I am beyond honored to be doing the same work Congresswoman Shirley Chisholm undertook when she founded the organization.

I have helped raise money for college scholarships with several non-profit groups. Whatever I can do to help give young people an opportunity to get a good college education, I am committed to doing. Anyone who has known me, even for a short while, understands that I won't allow moss to grow under my feet. It's just not in my DNA.

You might be saying, "I thought your husband wanted you to stay at home more." Well, it is a blessing to have a husband as incredible as Ben is, who can see and appreciate the woman God created me to be. It would be a crime to try to dim my light by asking me to sit around the house when I can be out helping people, especially young people, make it in life who may not have a good start. I have a wonderful husband who understands me and encourages what I do. What makes us work is his way of partnering with me in all of my endeavors. I thank God for Mr. Bennie Harris, aka, Honey.

I believe that making a difference in the lives of others is the best reward one can receive in life. I have received so many awards and certificates that I had to buy a huge binder to place them in. This poor little girl from Jayess, Mississippi, became a scientist and a community activist! All I can say is "With God, all things are possible."

CHAPTER EIGHT

WHEN YOU LEAST EXPECT IT

You've heard the old saying "out of the blue," haven't you? It usually refers to an unforeseen, remarkable, or surprising occurrence that happens when you least expect it. It could be a real good thing, like going to the dry cleaner's to pick up your laundry, and *out of the blue*, you bump into a really nice person who may one day become your spouse. Or, a dear, old friend drops by *out of the blue* for a friendly visit. But the saying could also bear an unexpected announcement one would prefer not to receive. In 2017, I was the recipient of one such *out of the blue* announcement.

I used to work out quite a bit. Even when I worked at Chevron, I went to the gym every day and was very conscientious about my weight and how I looked. I remember my doctor mentioning once that we should always be attuned to our bodies. If you notice there's anything different going on, you should say something. This thought always remains in the back of my mind.

And it was on my mind when I started having little muscle spasms in my tummy. The pain wasn't bad, but it was annoying. My stomach was cramping just a little on my right side. I'd had a colonoscopy about six months prior, but I still decided to go see my gastroenterologist, Dr. Chirag Patel. However, something as simple as making an appointment became very difficult. After checking my records, the receptionist reminded me that I'd just had a colonoscopy six months ago and went on to say that I didn't really need to have another one unless something major had occurred. I told the young lady I was having stomach cramps.

On July 12, 2017, Dr. Patel examined me again. During the examination, he noticed a little red bump right above my buttocks that resembled a strawberry. He pressed on it and asked me if it hurt. I told him it didn't. He then asked me how long the bump had been there. I told him I didn't know. He asked me for my phone so he could take a picture of it for me. I still have that picture on my phone today. I couldn't identify why the bump was there, other than maybe it was connected to the stomach pain. After I got dressed, Dr. Patel returned to the exam room and said, "Take this note over to Torrance Memorial Hospital. Go in immediately!" He said, "Go straight to the ER and give them this note." Right then I started wondering what in the world was going on! He then said, "Go now!" I left Dr. Patel's office and went to Torrance Memorial, which is less than one mile from his office.

After he had pressed on the affected area, my temperature started to rise. It had been perfectly normal when I walked into his office, but it had increased to 101 degrees. That is why he had me rush to the hospital. By the time I had arrived at the ER, my temperature had risen to 103 degrees. As you can imagine, I became frantic. I didn't understand what was going on. Within half an hour, I was in surgery. I didn't get a chance to tell my husband or anyone. I gave the hospital staff Bennie's contact information and was prepped for surgery!

The nurses started my IV and gave me everything I needed. The doctor told me that I had an abscess underneath my skin. If it were to burst, my blood stream would be poisoned, or I'd experience eminent death. Aggressive treatment was needed! I was petrified being there alone. Here I was, going into surgery, not knowing if I would come out of it alive.

I was in surgery for almost three and a half hours, and I was in intensive care for thirteen days. I shall never forget my room number: 4131, a room with a view. I could see small aircrafts take off and land over the Palos Verdes Peninsula. To my surprise, four of my doctors visited my room every single day to check on me while I was in the ICU. One of them said to me, "Normally, when I do surgery on a patient and they are doing okay, I never see them again. But you, I have to come in and see every day." Then he asked, "Why is that?" I replied, "YOU ALL LOVE ME." He let out a big, hearty laugh with a smile. Each one of the doctors eventually peeped in on me to say hello. I want to pause right here and thank these doctors: Dr. Patel, Dr. Mannan, Dr. McKissock, Dr. Eltawil, Dr. Atamdede, Dr. Milefchik, and Dr. McKinnell.

I had twenty-four-hour, around-the-clock care. I couldn't get out of bed because of the extent of my wound. They didn't want it to get infected, so I was situated right across the hall from the nurses' station, where they could get to me quickly. The staff came in to dress the wound three times a day. They had to keep a close eye on me to make sure I was healing properly. The wound had to heal from the inside out. If it had started healing from the outside, the surgeon would have to reopen the wound. This was the most challenging experience of my life.

After thirteen days in the ICU, I was able to go home. With the type of insurance I had, a nurse came in once a day to pack the wound. One thing my insurance company wanted me to do was allow them to train a family member to pack the wound. I had one of the highest and best plans offered, so I exclaimed "Absolutely not!" I have insurance, and I insist on using it! A nurse came in for six months to pack my wound.

One thing I found out through this is that you have certain rights, and you have to fight for them. A lot of times with surgeries, the insurance companies want to get you in and out of the hospital so they can have the hospital room for someone else. I was in a room that cost $10,000 a day, but I did not have to pay anything. My medical bills were close to $200,000, and I was so grateful that I had that Advance Insurance because I would have had to pay 20 percent of everything if I didn't.

I tell people, "You may not think you need insurance, but you do. You must protect yourself from unforeseen circumstances." In a million years, I never would have thought I would go through such a harrowing experience. I'm grateful I was covered. After having that surgery, I began sharing my experience and discovered there are many people in the world suffering from the same condition I had. But they don't talk about it because they are embarrassed or ashamed. I've had several friends tell me they went through the same thing. I asked them "Why didn't you tell me or want to talk about it?" Some people who find the sore on their bodies think it's a cold sore and that it will go away after a few days. Or, they think it's like a blister, and they can pop it. It is not wise to do that, as it creates other issues.

It took quite a while for me to recover after surgery. I had to stay in the house, I couldn't ride in a car, I could not drive, and I could not even sit down because of the size and location of the wound. I had to go through therapy, and I spent nine months in bed. While I was confined to my bedroom, my husband and kids waited on me hand and foot. When I was finally allowed to walk down the stairs, it was hard for me at first. You'd be surprised at the muscles we use every day that we take for granted. Every step that we make affects other parts of our bodies.

I've always believed in God and the Bible. Circumstances like the one I had can cause us to be introspective if we allow it. I had time to think about a lot of things. I was always rushing, just running and running. I discovered I needed to stop, reflect, and spend some much-needed time with my inner self. I'm really great at putting other people's needs first and putting off things I need to do for myself.

During that time, I reaffirmed my love for God. When I talk to people, I tell them that no one can say anything to make me doubt God and what He can do. His grace and mercy will always see you through. I know that all we need is faith the size of a mustard seed! We have to trust in Him. I still do today. I was brought up to be very religious, so it wasn't hard for me to realize that God is God, and He will do what He says He will do.

Many days I was alone as my family went about doing what their lives required. I'd be in the bedroom reading or lying there in pain. I took many different powerful pain pills and slept a lot. I did not become addicted to any of the pain meds, thank God! Toward the end of my healing, I started reducing the dosage. On the days that I didn't have pain, I didn't take the pills at all.

My husband was very loving and kind during this process. He would walk up and down the stairs of our home at least ten times a day. He made sure everything I needed was within reach, and he fixed breakfast, lunch, and dinner. I am eternally thankful for the time he spent taking such good care of me. He put off doing a lot of things just so he could stay home and make me feel special. This experience brought us closer together and strengthened our relationship. He honored his vow to be there "in sickness and in health." I will be forever grateful to him, to God, and to the kids. My husband stood by me, and that made me happier than I can express.

My girls were right there with me whenever they could be. Nakita is a nurse, so she would stay in the bedroom next to mine, and Shanta, in between her business dealings, would come in and make calls for me. I got a lot of phone calls, so she didn't get much sleep. Family in Mississippi and surrounding areas were always calling to check on me. I received a ton of get-well cards, some from people I didn't think would take time to mail a card. I have put the cards away because they have become keepsakes that help me realize there are people out there who really do care. They may not say it, but when you are in need, they step up to the plate. Some even brought food over and took time out of their busy schedules to visit with me.

Now, I'm always looking at my body to make sure there are no spots—red or any other color. I check my hip area constantly because of my experience. I hope my story will encourage others to keep checking their bodies, too. I could have died. I never thought something like that would happen to me. Sometimes I'm still shocked. I've spent a year and a half sharing my story with people. I don't talk about it as much as I did right after it happened, but when I can, I tell people to be attuned to their bodies. If you don't feel good, take the time to go to the doctor.

It's been two and a half years since my ordeal, and I wanted to make sure I didn't wait too long before having another colonoscopy. When I called recently to make an appointment, the nurse said, "You're not supposed to come back for 10 years." I said, "Are you joking? You have to be kidding. No, I want an appointment as soon as possible!" When she asked me if I was having any issues, I replied, "Yes, I am. The issue is that I have insurance." After I had that surgery, I was told to have a colonoscopy every two years. We must be diligent and persistent when it comes to our health. The doctors that took care of me told me I saved my own life by being persistent.

I THANK GOD I'M STILL HERE!!! I am truly grateful and thankful to God to still be in the land of the living. I am thankful for His MERCY and FAVOR. I'm thankful to the Lord for the team of doctors at Torrance Memorial Hospital, for their wisdom and quick thinking that contributed to saving my life. I'm so grateful for my loving and praying husband, who never left my side, exemplifying what true love is! I'm thankful to my daughters who also stayed by my side every day, helping, praying, and simply being present. I'm also thankful for my sweet sister Johnnie, who spent nights with me to keep me company and pray for me!! I am grateful for my grandkids, who loved and cared for their Granny!! I'm thankful to my Pastor, Joseph C. Robinson, and First Lady, Andrea, and the church members for coming to sit and pray with me after my surgery! I'm thankful for every friend that visited and/or called to pray with me and lift my spirits up. There were so many lovely cards, flowers, and teddy bears. I am truly overwhelmed with emotions and gratitude for how GOOD God is for blessing me with another chance at life!! How generous God is to bless me with such awesome family and friends. I will never be able to thank Him enough. But believe me; I will try my BEST!

Listen to your body, fight for your health when something doesn't feel right, and demand the attention you need. You just might save your life!

CHAPTER NINE

NEVER GIVE UP! A MOTHER'S MOTIVATION

As I've said before, my mother is the best thing in the world to me. My mom has always gone above and beyond for her family. So, after I started working, I put her on my payroll and began sending her and my stepdad $200 a month to thank them for everything they had done to get me through college and help me through the rough times. I found out later that Mom was giving her half of the money to my sister Lorean's daughter, Summer, and my stepfather was giving his half to Lorean's son, Michael. Both my mom and step-dad had big hearts.

I really wanted my mother to take that money and do something for herself, like buy a new dress or some nice perfume or treat herself to something special. But mom stayed true to form and continued helping others in their time of need, even if she had to do without. She is the most selfless person I know and is such a beautiful example to follow. Her example still teaches me how to operate in the world with kindness, selflessness, and generosity.

Mom is ninety-one years old now. She is frail these days, and it's difficult for her to do certain things, talking being one of them. When I do go home to visit and I see her in such a fragile state, it breaks my heart. As soon as she sees me, she recognizes me and calls out my name. I run to hug her, lay my head on her chest, and smother her with kisses. When the nurse puts her to bed in the evening, I always go in like a big baby and snuggle with her. When she wakes up in the morning, I'm there to place kisses on her face, give her a big hug, and greet her with a good morning smile. Sometimes she manages to gain the strength to hug me back.

Of course, I now wish even more that I didn't live three thousand miles away from her. I feel that if I'd been closer I could have learned a lot more from her. So, now all the memories, notes, and artifacts I have received from her over the years are like precious jewels to me. Since I was about 10 years ago, I'd sit right next to Mom with a pen and pad and ask her to share something she had never shared before, and I would write. The things she has shared are what I reflect on now. I am extremely grateful to God for the time I've had with her and for our relationship. That is why I can never forget her or her accomplishments.

My mother had only a fifth-grade education, but she has accomplished a lot through the years, surpassing many who have gone on to obtain the highest degrees of education. Listed below are the numerous awards she has been honored with through the years.

EULA LEE BROWN-HILL SERVICE AWARDS

1958	Florian Manor- Certificate of Service- "Grateful recognition of 5 years of dedication, loyalty, understanding, performance, and untiring efforts while serving the residents of our facility and the State of Mississippi"
1988	June Heritage Manor of Columbia- Employee of the Month
1991	Certificate- "Successfully completed all course work required and hereby receives the designation of CERTIFIED NURSING ASSISTANT"
1991	Mississippi State Department of Health- Division of Health Facilities- "Licensure and certification- successfully completed competency evaluation program for nurse aide certification in long-term care and is listed on the Nurse Aide Registry, in

the State of Mississippi" Certificate Number #A07991

1999 "Columbia Health and Rehabilitation Center certificate in appreciation for your hard work and devotion"

2002 Annual Marion County Black History Celebration-Memorial Award

2003 The 16th Annual Marion County Black History Celebration

2004 The 17th Annual Marion County- Memorial Award

2005 The 18th Annual Black History Award- "Eula Lee Hill from Columbia Re-Hab, with 37½ years"

2005 "Courage in the Face of Adversity for selfless assistance and dedication to the residents, staff, and community of Columbia Health and Rehab during Hurricane Katrina"

2006 Nurse's Aide Award- "Certificate of Appreciation for Outstanding Service"

2008 Eula Lee Hill "55 years of service at Columbia Health and Rehab Center" Retired

"Never give up" was her charge to all of her children. I pass these words on to you. I want to lift you up and impart the goodness that my mother deposited into me over the years into you. I am writing this book, but my mother's voice has influenced every word. Please understand that you are going to have obstacles in life. Your path isn't always going to be clear. You have to allow yourself to make errors in life and realize that making mistakes doesn't mean it's over. It is an opportunity to learn, mature, and grow. Remember to remain focused. Even God says life will not be easy, but your outcome depends on how positive you are. So, don't be afraid to make mistakes; they don't define you. When you fall, just get up, dust yourself off, and keep pushing forward!

Although I'd always had dreams of going to college, I was afraid it may be too difficult. Because I missed a lot of school to help my family when I was growing up, I thought I'd missed a lot of education. I even told my mother that I didn't think I would make it because it was too hard. I was ready to throw in the towel and come home, but she said, "No! You cannot do that. Remember all the things you've learned about life. You cannot give up!" She kept pointing to her head and repeating to all of us over and over again: "Once you get the knowledge in your head, no one can take that from you. You have to keep going; you have to weather the storm!"

Thinking back over it all right now, I feel it's the best advice she could have given me. Students approach me now and tell me about the hardships they are facing. And guess what I tell them. Yes, you've got that right! I tell them that they can't give up; they must stay focused.

Writing a book about my life while also gracing its cover is a profound moment for me. I am grateful for the pioneering path God chose for me. Being the first woman to break the gender barrier in a male-dominated sector was just short of miraculous. I hope the thirty-eight plus years I worked at the Chevron Corporation have served to create a firm foundation within the company upon which all ethnic and gender groups can stand to make their own marks in history and in the evolution of science and mankind. I pray that men and women of color of all ages, both young and old, find my story to be a symbol of hope and inspiration.

I believe that, with God, all things are possible. Because of this, I am able to raise money to help underserved students who are less fortunate. With the help and support of willing donors, we are able to help children who have achieved a 2.5 (C+) grade-point average that are eager to wedge their foot in the door to receive a college education. I was that student with a B- grade-point average, but someone gave me a chance. I would not be in the position I am today had it not been for the help of others. Using the gifts and talents we are born with carries great weight and goes a long way. Not one of us was placed on this earth to sit and just take up space. We have been created to use what we've been given to make this world stronger, better, and kinder, undergirded with love. The sum total of all our gifts and talents, when knitted together, can create something brilliant and life-giving; we are stronger and better together. It doesn't matter where you start but rather how you apply what you have to achieve your best, so you can leave a legacy behind that can live on forever!

NOTES

Chapter 2:

1 Warren Kulo. *Study Finds Mississippi Is the Worst State in Which to Live.* https://www.gulflive.com/mississippi-press-news/2015/11/study_finds_mississippi_is_the.html.

2 Thomas C. Frohlich and Michael B. Sauter. America's Best and Worst States to Live In. https://247wallst.com/special-report/2015/11/23/most-livable-states/.

3 ibid.

For Speaking Engagements, Book Signings,
Appearances, and Interviews...

CONTACT

ALENE BROWN HARRIS

✉ A.harris1898@yahoo.com

f facebook.com/ALENECFAA

○ @alenebharris

🐦 @AharrisC21